# Learning Disabilities

**Diseases and Disorders**

ReferencePoint
Press™

San Diego, CA

# Select* books in the Compact Research series include:

## Current Issues

Abortion
Animal Experimentation
Biomedical Ethics
Cloning
Conflict in the Middle East
The Death Penalty
Energy Alternatives
Free Speech
Genetic Engineering
Global Warming and
　Climate Change
Gun Control
Illegal Immigration

Islam
Media Violence
National Security
Nuclear Weapons and
　Security
Obesity
School Violence
Stem Cells
Terrorist Attacks
U.S. Border Control
Video Games
World Energy Crisis

## Diseases and Disorders

ADHD
Alzheimer's Disease
Anorexia
Autism
Bipolar Disorders
Hepatitis

HPV
Meningitis
Phobias
Sexually Transmitted
　Diseases

## Drugs

Alcohol
Antidepressants
Club Drugs
Cocaine and Crack
Hallucinogens
Heroin
Inhalants

Marijuana
Methamphetamine
Nicotine and Tobacco
Performance-Enhancing
　Drugs
Prescription Drugs
Steroids

## Energy and the Environment

Biofuels
Deforestation
Fossil Fuels

Hydrogen Power
Solar Power
Wind Power

*For a complete list of titles please visit www.referencepointpress.com.

# Learning Disabilities

by Peggy J. Parks

**Diseases and Disorders**

ReferencePoint
Press®

San Diego, CA

© 2010 ReferencePoint Press, Inc.

**For more information, contact:**
ReferencePoint Press, Inc.
PO Box 27779
San Diego, CA 92198
www.ReferencePointPress.com

Picture credits:
Cover: iStockphoto.com
Maury Aaseng: 33–35, 47–50, 62–63, 76–78
Landov: 13, 19

LIBRARY OF CONGRESS CATALOGING-IN-PUBLICATION DATA

Parks, Peggy J., 1951–
    Learning disabilities / by Peggy J. Parks.
        p. cm. — (Compact research series)
    Includes bibliographical references and index.
    ISBN-13: 978-1-60152-077-7 (hardback)
    ISBN-10: 1-60152-077-8 (hardback)
    1. Learning disabilities—Juvenile literature. 2. Learning disabled—Education—Juvenile literature. I. Title.
    LC4704.P36    2009
    371.9—dc22
                                                            2009013445

# Contents

# Foreword

As modern civilization continues to evolve, its ability to create, store, distribute, and access information expands exponentially. The explosion of information from all media continues to increase at a phenomenal rate. By 2020 some experts predict the worldwide information base will double every 73 days. While access to diverse sources of information and perspectives is paramount to any democratic society, information alone cannot help people gain knowledge and understanding. Information must be organized and presented clearly and succinctly in order to be understood. The challenge in the digital age becomes not the creation of information, but how best to sort, organize, enhance, and present information.

ReferencePoint Press developed the *Compact Research* series with this challenge of the information age in mind. More than any other subject area today, researching current issues can yield vast, diverse, and unqualified information that can be intimidating and overwhelming for even the most advanced and motivated researcher. The *Compact Research* series offers a compact, relevant, intelligent, and conveniently organized collection of information covering a variety of current topics ranging from illegal immigration and deforestation to diseases such as anorexia and meningitis.

The series focuses on three types of information: objective single-author narratives, opinion-based primary source quotations, and facts and statistics. The clearly written objective narratives provide context and reliable background information. Primary source quotes are carefully selected and cited, exposing the reader to differing points of view. And facts and statistics sections aid the reader in evaluating perspectives. Presenting these key types of information creates a richer, more balanced learning experience.

For better understanding and convenience, the series enhances information by organizing it into narrower topics and adding design features that make it easy for a reader to identify desired content. For example, in *Compact Research: Illegal Immigration*, a chapter covering the economic impact of illegal immigration has an objective narrative explaining the various ways the economy is impacted, a balanced section of numerous primary source quotes on the topic, followed by facts and full-color illustrations to encourage evaluation of contrasting perspectives.

The ancient Roman philosopher Lucius Annaeus Seneca wrote, "It is quality rather than quantity that matters." More than just a collection of content, the *Compact Research* series is simply committed to creating, finding, organizing, and presenting the most relevant and appropriate amount of information on a current topic in a user-friendly style that invites, intrigues, and fosters understanding.

# Learning Disabilities at a Glance

## Definition

The term *learning disabilities* refers to a variety of disorders that involve specific challenges such as reading, writing, listening, speaking, concentrating, and/or solving mathematics problems.

## Prevalence

According to the National Center for Learning Disabilities, 15 million children, adolescents, and adults in the United States are affected by one or more learning disabilities.

## Signs and Symptoms

Preschool children with learning disabilities may have trouble learning the alphabet, speaking new words or sentences, learning numbers and counting, identifying colors, and understanding questions. Children with mild to moderate learning disabilities are often not diagnosed until they start school.

## Causes

Scientists believe the brains of learning-disabled people are wired differently, although they do not know why. Possible contributing factors include genetic influences; brain development before birth; mothers who smoked, drank alcohol, or took drugs while they were pregnant; and exposure to environmental poisons such as lead or mercury.

## Diagnosis

Learning disabilities are diagnosed following evaluations that measure speech and language as well as intellectual evaluations that test verbal and nonverbal skills. A disturbing number of learning disability cases go undiagnosed or are misdiagnosed.

## Treatment

The specific treatment varies based on the type of learning disability someone has and often involves specialized education programs that build on the person's strengths and help compensate for his or her shortcomings.

## Long-Term Prognosis

With the right education and treatment, many learning-disabled people overcome their disabilities and go on to earn college degrees and become successful in life.

# Overview

**❝Children with learning disabilities are not 'dumb' or 'lazy.' In fact, they usually have average or above average intelligence. Their brains just process information differently.❞**

—National Dissemination Center for Children with Disabilities, an organization that provides information on issues such as child and youth disabilities, programs and services, and special education laws.

**❝A learning disability doesn't have anything to do with a person's intelligence—after all, such successful people as Walt Disney, Alexander Graham Bell, and Winston Churchill all had learning disabilities.❞**

—D'Arcy Lyness, a child and adolescent psychologist from Wayne, Pennsylvania.

There was a time not so long ago when children who had trouble reading, writing, listening, understanding, or communicating in accordance with their grade levels were labeled as "mentally impaired" or "retarded." Many developed normally up through their preschool years, but once they entered grade school, their ability to learn lagged significantly behind their peers. *What is wrong with him?* teachers and parents wondered. *Why won't she try harder and apply herself? Why won't he pay attention in class? Why is she being so lazy?* Such perceptions were often grossly inaccurate, as the children *were* applying themselves, they *were* trying, and they were *not* being lazy. Yet no matter how much effort they put forth, no matter how hard they tried, their progress was derailed by learning disabilities over which they had no control. Sadly, their sense of failure was often reinforced by parents and teachers, the very people who had the greatest amount of influence over them and who had the power to help them overcome the learning struggles that plagued them day after day. Author and special education professor Robert Evert Cimera explains the profound impact this negative experience can have on a learning-disabled child:

> You see, kids with learning disabilities are limited more by how people treat them than they are by their actual learning problems. In essence, they become what people think they are—slow, stupid, unmotivated, dull . . . add whatever words you like. . . . Teach your child that she can succeed, and she probably will. Teach your child that he is stupid and that he will never make anything out of his life, and he probably won't. It is that simple.[1]

## What Are Learning Disabilities?

The term *learning disabilities* (LD) refers to a variety of disorders that involve specific challenges such as reading, writing, listening, speaking, concentrating, and/or solving mathematics problems. A learning disability is not a diagnosis in the same way as an illness or disease with a known cause and typical symptoms. Rather, as the *Learning Disabilities Sourcebook* explains:

> LD is a broad term that covers a pool of possible causes, symptoms, treatments, and outcomes. . . . Not all learning problems are necessarily learning disabilities. Many children are simply slower in developing certain skills. Because children show natural differences in their rate of development, sometimes what seems to be a learning disability may simply be a delay in maturation. To be diagnosed as a learning disability, specific criteria must be met.[2]

The book goes on to say that learning disabilities are often referred to as a "hidden handicap" because they are not visible or obvious in the same way as physical disorders such paralysis or blindness. The authors write: "A learning disability doesn't disfigure or leave visible signs that would invite others to be understanding or offer support."[3]

## Types of Learning Disabilities

There are a number of different learning disabilities, each with its own corresponding characteristics. Although some people suffer from more than one type, many people are deficient in a single set of skills while they excel at others, as psychologist Arlyn Roffman explains: "One of the interesting things about LD is how [diverse] it is. A person can be an abysmal speller but be a strong reader. Or a brilliant mathematician but weak in social skills. Or very social but unable to independently organize his belongings or schoolwork."[4]

Many health-care professionals say that the most common type of learning disability is dyslexia, which is a general term used to describe reading and language-based problems. According to the International Dyslexia Association, of all the children who have learning disabilities, an estimated 80 percent suffer from dyslexia. Many dyslexics also suffer from dysgraphia, whereby they struggle with spelling, penmanship, and the ability to express words and thoughts in writing. Those who have dyscalculia may possess average or above-average language, reading, and writing skills but have difficulties with abstract concepts such as time and direction and struggle with the logic and problem-solving required by mathematics. A relatively unknown learning disability is dysnomia, which is a memory retrieval disorder. People with dysnomia have severe difficulties recalling words from memory, which makes it hard for them to express what they want to say both verbally and in written form.

> "A learning disability is not a diagnosis in the same way as an illness or disease with a known cause and typical symptoms."

There are also learning disabilities in which people have problems socializing with others and have a difficult time making friends. Alison Rhodes is a woman from Connecticut whose son has this type of learning disability. She explains the struggles he faces: "When Spencer is around other boys his age, his disability is painfully obvious. I often end up crying when I see him with a group of other boys and he can't keep up a conversation and they don't include him in games."[5]

*The term* learning disabilities *refers to a variety of disorders that involve specific challenges such as reading, writing, listening, speaking, concentrating, and/or solving mathematics problems. Many students with learning disabilities do not test well. These high school students are taking a practice exam.*

Cimera, the special education professor, has a learning disability known as dysphasia. It affects people's capacity to understand language and correctly process what they are told. He says that for those who suffer from dysphasia, processing auditory stimuli is an ongoing, and often daunting, challenge. He shares what it is like to live with the disability and describes the opinions that others tend to form when they observe someone who has it. "Imagine having this problem. Think about how it would affect you and your life. People would probably think that you were spacey, inattentive, or unmotivated to remember things."[6] Cimera adds that erroneous perceptions about dysphasia and other learning disabilities are widespread even today. People often jump to the conclusion that those who are learning disabled are doomed to a life of ignorance, have little or no hope of getting a college education, and are destined to work in the most menial of jobs—if they are employable at all. Cimera himself experienced this, as he explains: "Where would I be if I listened to those of my teachers who said that I wasn't 'college material' or that I didn't have 'what it takes' to be a writer?"[7]

> **Many health-care professionals say that the most common type of learning disability is dyslexia, which is a general term used to describe reading and language-based problems.**

Cimera is a shining example of how successful learning-disabled people can be if their problems are correctly diagnosed, they are given the right support, and they have the motivation to work hard to overcome their learning hurdles by focusing on their abilities rather than their *dis*abilities. After being diagnosed with dysphasia when he was in college, Cimera beat the odds (and showed his detractors how wrong they were) by finishing college and earning a PhD. He went on to write eight books and is now a special education professor at Kent State University. He works extensively with children who have learning disabilities. Yet even now he struggles because of what he went through as he was growing up. "What affected me most in life," he writes, "wasn't my difficulty in learning auditory information. What affected me the most was the feeling that I was a loser. . . . Even with all of the many wonderful things that I have accomplished, I still feel like the little kid who was constantly made fun of and teased. I still feel like I can't do anything right. Even now, on occasion, I get depressed."[8]

## Is ADHD a Learning Disability?

Articles and books on learning disabilities often include references to attention deficit hyperactivity disorder, or ADHD, because it is so common among children and adults. Yet even though learning disabilities and ADHD are related, they are not the same, as special education teacher Darcy Andries explains: "A common misconception about attention deficit hyperactivity disorder . . . is that it is a learning disability. Confusion about the two occur because ADHD can affect learning and because as many as thirty percent of people with ADHD also have a learning disability."[9]

Andries says the biggest difference between the disorders is that even though a student with a learning disability has a deficit in one or two areas, he or she will generally perform at or above average in other areas, whereas students with ADHD have problems with *all* cognitive functions. She uses an analogy to describe this:

> Imagine the "normal" brain as a room with all the lights on. A learning disability will turn off one or two of the lamps in the room, leaving some areas dark while others are still bright. However, ADHD dims all the lights in the room; it affects the person all the time, not just when they are performing specific cognitive functions (like reading). A student with both ADHD and a learning disability will have the lights dim throughout the room, with one or two areas significantly darker.[10]

## Prevalence of Learning Disabilities

Learning disabilities are extremely common. They affect children and adults of all ages, races, religions, walks of life, and income levels. According to the National Center for Learning Disabilities, 15 million children, adolescents, and adults in the United States are affected by one or more learning disabilities. The Centers for Disease Control and Prevention (CDC) states that 4.7 million children from age 3 to 17 had a learning disability during 2006.

## Do Learning Disabilities Affect Boys More Often than Girls?

Many health-care professionals say that boys have learning disabilities, especially dyslexia, far more often than girls. A July 2008 report by the CDC showed that among students aged 6 to 17, boys are about twice as likely as girls to have both ADHD and learning disabilities and about one-third more likely than girls to have learning disabilities without ADHD. This is a controversial issue, though, because not everyone agrees that gender is a factor in who suffers from learning disabilities. According to the National Association of Special Education Teachers

(NASET), equal numbers of boys and girls suffer from dyslexia, but for unknown reasons many girls' learning disabilities are not identified and therefore not treated. Some researchers, NASET states, suggest that the higher prevalence among males is due to "referral bias," meaning that when males exhibit academic problems, they are more readily referred to special education classes because they are more apt to be disruptive in the classroom.

## Warning Signs and Symptoms

There is no one sign, symptom, or set of signs and symptoms, that applies to everyone with learning disabilities. One of the earliest signs in a child with a severe learning disability is delays in achieving certain developmental milestones, or falling short of what is considered normal for his or her age. In preschool children this may include difficulties in learning the alphabet, speaking new words or sentences, learning numbers and counting, identifying colors, understanding questions, and a lack of interest in storytelling. Other possible indicators in young children include motor delays such as clumsiness or awkwardness and the inability (or seeming unwillingness) to follow directions.

Children with mild to moderate learning disabilities are often not diagnosed until they start school. By kindergarten or first grade, they may begin to exhibit problems with language, memory, spelling and writing, concentration, and/or reading comprehension. They may also have socialization problems that impede their ability to make friends. They often do not get jokes or sarcasm (by teachers or classmates), and they tend to get confused about why they are supposed to follow rules such as standing in line, taking turns, and waiting until someone finishes speaking before they talk. Social worker Gary Direnfeld describes the typical symptoms of a learning disability that affect social skills:

> Even though learning disabilities and ADHD are related, they are not the same.

> The child may act the class clown. The child may prefer to hang out with the adults. The child likely uses phrases,

innuendo, jokes or sarcasm heard from others, but uses them inappropriately, at the wrong time, with the wrong persons. The child has a poor sense of boundaries, will interrupt, walk in on others or take or use things without asking. The child may have few friends and those the child does have are similar in nature. The child may be frequently scolded or punished. The child struggles at school and may be bullied.[11]

## What Causes Learning Disabilities?

The exact cause of learning disabilities is unknown, as Cimera explains: "Researchers really don't know what causes learning disabilities. However, current thought is that learning disabilities stem from differences in how the brain processes information. This isn't to say that people with learning disabilities have defective brains. They don't. They just perceive things differently."[12] Yet even though scientists cannot pinpoint one cause, or even a distinct collection of causes, certain factors are believed to be linked to the development of learning disabilities. These include genetic influences (some learning disabilities are known to run in families); brain development before and during birth; low birth weight, including premature birth; mothers who smoked, drank alcohol, or took drugs while they were pregnant; poor nutrition; and exposure to environmental poisons such as lead or other toxic heavy metals.

## Diagnosis of Learning Disabilities

In order for learning disabilities to be properly diagnosed, all other possible causes (including medical problems or mental retardation) must be ruled out. For this reason, learning disabilities are sometimes referred to as a "diagnosis of exclusion." According to psychiatrists Afia Ali and Ian Hall, what are thought to be learning disabilities may actually be side effects of health problems such as epilepsy; hearing or vision loss; extreme weight fluctuations, from being underweight and malnourished to obese; mental disorders such as schizophrenia, bipolar disorder, and depression; and ADHD.

Learning disabilities are typically identified by regular education teachers who note marked discrepancies between a child's perceived potential and actual performance. If a learning disability is suspected, the first step is usually a complete physical examination so that all other potential contributors can be ruled out. Next comes evaluations that measure speech and language, as well as intellectual evaluations that test verbal and nonverbal skills. Once a child's specific learning disability (or disabilities) has been determined, an appropriate treatment program is developed by a team of educators, with input from the parents.

> "One of the earliest signs in a child with a severe learning disability is delays in achieving certain developmental milestones, or falling short of what is considered normal for his or her age."

Unfortunately, a disturbing number of learning disabilities remain undiagnosed. Some people go through their whole lives wondering why they have problems learning or concentrating, often suffering through degradation by parents and teachers, being told they lack intelligence, feeling like no matter how hard they try, they cannot seem to do anything right, believing that they are stupid and beyond help—when the real problem is a learning disability that they never knew they had.

## Treatment of Learning Disabilities

The earlier a learning disability is diagnosed and treatment begins, the more significant progress a child can make. Treatment focuses on helping him or her learn ways to cope with the learning disability and overcome it, and the specific treatment program varies based on the type of disorder. All U.S. states are required to provide a free and individual education for children with special needs, including learning disabilities, even during the preschool years. Educators develop individualized educational plans (IEPs) that specify what services will be provided to the child and by whom, and that focus on the child's unique strengths and talents. To address self-esteem issues, psychological counseling and behavioral therapy are often recommended to work in tandem with special educational classes. For some learning disabilities, medications may be prescribed to help the child focus and concentrate, although many health-care professionals say that the effectiveness of such drugs is questionable.

## Can People Overcome Learning Disabilities?

Many successful people have lived with learning disabilities for much of their lives and have learned strategies and methods of overcoming them. One example is Gavin Newsom, who is the mayor of San Francisco. Newsom, who was diagnosed with dyslexia when he was in the fifth grade, says that he was "terrible in school."[13] He found reading and

*Gavin Newsom, the mayor of San Francisco, was diagnosed with dyslexia when he was in the fifth grade. Despite his professional success, he still struggles with the disability.*

writing to be a constant struggle, had to stay after school three days a week to get extra help from teachers, and dreaded any occasion when he was required to speak before a group. Newsom admits that he still gets nervous during public speaking appearances even though they are a regular part of his job. Another drawback of Newsom's dyslexia is that he has to read newspaper articles at least two times in order to understand them fully, and he is known for making plentiful spelling mistakes when he writes memos to members of his staff. In an April 2004 speech at a private school for students with learning disabilities, Newsom shared his personal experience with the group: "I still have dyslexia—it doesn't magically go away. . . . But it's OK. It gets a lot easier if you work hard." He had some encouraging words for those who shared his struggle with learning disabilities: "You're going to be better people because of the academic struggles you have right now. . . . There is nothing in this world you guys can't accomplish—I promise you that."[14]

> " In order for learning disabilities to be properly diagnosed, all other possible causes (including medical problems or mental retardation) must be ruled out. "

## Can Learning Disabilities Be Cured?

An overwhelming number of health-care professionals agree that there is no cure for learning disabilities, nor do people outgrow them. Those who successfully overcome their learning hurdles do so not by "getting over" the disabilities as they would an illness, but rather by learning to compensate for them. The National Dissemination Center for Children with Disabilities explains: "Children with LD can be high achievers and can be taught ways to get around the learning disability. With the right help, children with LD can and do learn successfully."[15]

Scientists continue to study learning disabilities in the hope of gaining a better understanding of their cause, including why some children suffer from them when so many others do not. It is their hope that this research will potentially lead to preventative measures and perhaps eventually a cure.

# From Hopeless to Hope

Once thought to be a sign of insurmountable mental impairment, learning disabilities are now much better understood and are known to be cognitive challenges that can be overcome. With the right treatment plan, children with dyslexia can and do become proficient readers, and those with other types of learning disabilities learn to compensate for them while developing their own unique talents and skills. In the process, many learning-disabled people become more successful than they ever dreamed. Can someone be cured of learning disabilities? Most experts say no, that is not possible—at least for now. But through hope, support, encouragement, and hard work, many people manage to overcome learning disabilities and live life to its fullest.

# What Are Learning Disabilities?

66A learning disability is a *neurobiological disorder;* people with LD have brains that learn differently because of differences in brain structure and/or function.99

—Kyla Boyse, a registered nurse from Ann Arbor, Michigan.

66People with learning disabilities have difficulty taking information in through the senses and processing the information with accuracy to the brain. The information becomes scrambled, like a short circuit, a distorted radio signal, or a fuzzy television picture.99

—Georgia's Assistive Technology Act Program, which seeks to increase access to assistive technology devices and services for Georgians of all ages and disabilities.

In 1877 a German physician named Adolf Kussmaul published an article in which he described the unusual disorder of one of his adult patients. Although the man was of average intelligence and had no vision or speech problems, he suffered from a severe reading deficiency that Kussmaul referred to as "word blindness." His article stated:

> In medical literature we find cases recorded as aphasia which should not properly be designated by this name, since the patients were still able to express their thoughts by speech and writing. They had not lost the power either of speaking or of writing; they were no longer able, however, although the hearing was perfect, to understand the words which they heard, or, although the sight was perfect, to read the written words which they saw.[16]

Throughout the following years other physicians observed and wrote about patients who were intelligent and expressed themselves well verbally, but who had severe deficiencies in reading. In 1887 German ophthalmologist Rudolf Berlin coined the term *dyslexia* to describe this particular reading disorder.

## A Movement Gains Strength

Even though physicians and scientists began writing about people with reading deficiencies in the 1800s, the problem remained a mystery for nearly a century. Learning-disabled students were commonly pronounced to be brain damaged or mentally retarded, and if they received any specialized education at all, they were usually put into classes for slow learners for whom academic success was thought to be impossible. As a result, most of these young people had no confidence in themselves and lived up (or rather, down) to the bleak expectations others had of them.

Fortunately, this began to change during the early 1960s. Growing numbers of parents were desperate to find services to help their special-needs children, many of whom had either been diagnosed as "perceptually handicapped" or "minimally brain damaged," but no such services existed. In order to raise awareness of their cause and to generate support for specialized education, in April 1963 a parent group hosted a conference in Chicago entitled Exploration into the Problems of the Perceptually Handicapped Child. A keynote speaker was Samuel Kirk, a psychologist who had extensive experience working with special-needs children. Kirk shared with the group the term *learning disabilities*, which

> Even though physicians and scientists began writing about people with reading deficiencies in the 1800s, the problem remained a mystery for nearly a century.

he had first introduced in his book *Educating Exceptional Children*. He explained that learning-disabled children were those with "disorders in development in language, speech, reading, and associated communication skills needed for social interaction," and then he described the students to whom the definition did not apply: "In this group, I do not include children who have sensory handicaps such as blindness or deafness, because we have methods of managing and training the deaf and the blind. I also exclude from this group children who have generalized mental retardation."[17] The parents who attended the conference found Kirk's talk to be inspirational as well as motivating—finally, someone understood the hurdles they were facing and believed there was hope for their children. The following January the parent group founded the Association for Children with Learning Disabilities (later changed to the Learning Disabilities Association of America) and began lobbying for their children to receive specialized help in school.

> **Many people, including adults as well as children, have poor reading skills, but that does not necessarily mean they are learning disabled.**

Over the following years awareness of learning disabilities grew at a rapid pace. In 1969 the U.S. Congress passed the Children with Specific Learning Disabilities Act, which marked the first time federal law mandated educational support services for learning-disabled children. More and more schools throughout the United States created special education programs that grouped students according to their individual needs and helped address their unique learning problems. In 1975, with congressional passage of the Education of All Handicapped Children Act, all students aged 3 to 21 with special needs were guaranteed a free and appropriate public education and the right to learn in regular classrooms along with students who were not learning disabled. Fifteen years later the law was revised to change the term *handicap* to *disability* and was renamed the Individuals with Disabilities Education Act (IDEA).

IDEA legislation has been revised several times over the years, and today learning disabilities are defined by IDEA as follows:

> The term "specific learning disability" means a disorder in 1 or more of the basic psychological processes involved in understanding or in using language, spoken or written, which disorder may manifest itself in the imperfect abil-

ity to listen, think, speak, read, write, spell, or do mathematical calculations. . . . [This] term includes such conditions as perceptual disabilities, brain injury, minimal brain dysfunction, dyslexia, and developmental aphasia. [The] term does not include a learning problem that is primarily the result of visual, hearing, or motor disabilities, of mental retardation, of emotional disturbance, or of environmental, cultural, or economic disadvantage.[18]

## The Struggles of Dyslexia

Many people, adults as well as children, have poor reading skills, but that does not necessarily mean they are learning disabled. Someone's reading ability can be affected by such factors as impaired vision, poor diet and nutrition, physical ailments, stress, the quality of education, and environment. It is important to note that those with dyslexia are not merely poor readers; they suffer from a disorder that Robert Cimera describes as "probably the most devastating to a person's academic development." The reason dyslexia is so debilitating is that reading plays such a fundamental role in people's daily lives, as Cimera explains: "Reading disabilities . . . are pretty far-reaching. They affect one's ability to get information out of a newspaper, order off a menu, follow the rules of the road, fill out a job application, and many, many other activities."[19]

> " Although it is a myth that people with dyslexia see words backward and read from right to left instead of left to right, many dyslexics do get letters mixed up, often inverting or reversing them. "

Actor Tom Cruise was diagnosed with dyslexia when he was seven years old, and he shares the frustration this caused throughout his life:

I'd try to concentrate on what I was reading, then I'd get to the end of the page and have very little memory of anything I'd read. I would go blank, feel anxious, nervous, bored, frustrated, dumb. I would get angry. My legs would actually hurt when I was studying. My head ached. All through school and well into my career, I felt like I had a secret. When I'd go to a new school, I wouldn't want the other kids to know about my learning disability.[20]

Cruise says that one of his fondest dreams was to become a pilot, and when he was making the movie *Top Gun*, he finally got the chance to make his dream come true. "I thought, 'This is the time to do it,' so I had a couple of lessons. But then I just blew it off. When people asked what happened, I told them I was too busy preparing for the film, just didn't have time. The truth is, I couldn't learn how to do it."[21]

One of the most common problems that many dyslexics share is difficulty decoding words on a page. They decode differently from normal readers, who look at words and instantaneously attach them to their meaning, a process known as associative thinking. If nondyslexic people see the word *automobile*, for instance, they automatically envision a car, and if they see the word *daffodil* they envision the perky yellow flower. But for people who have dyslexia, reading is not an associative process; it is a cognitive process that requires a great deal of effort. When dyslexics see words, nothing is automatic. They must first identify each letter, determine what words the letters are forming, and then associate the words with their meaning. This is true not only with long words but also with short, simple words,

> People with dysgraphia may be good readers and excel at speaking but struggle with spelling, have penmanship that no one can read, and be unable to transfer their thoughts into written form.

as Cimera writes: "[Dyslexics] are much like people who are learning a new language. They have to work a little harder to decode and comprehend what they see. They have to process each part of the word to make sense of the whole. They come across words like *the*, *and*, *of*, and so forth, and they have to give them meaning, which takes time and energy."[22]

Although it is a myth that people with dyslexia see words backward and read from right to left instead of left to right, many dyslexics do get letters mixed up, often inverting or reversing them. For example, they may see a *p* and mistake it for a *b, q,* or *d.* Other typical problems many dyslexics have involve seeing words swirling around on a page and words sliding out of place and mixing with other text so sentences make no sense. Closely associated with these reading difficulties are problems with comprehension. Since dyslexics cannot process words in the same way as other readers, understanding what they read can be an arduous task. Cimera uses the example of someone with dyslexia reading the sentence "It was a dark and stormy night," and he describes the complicated process the person would have to go through in order to understand what it means: "'It was' . . . that means the situation is in the past tense. So it isn't happening now. It happened a while ago. 'Dark' means black or hard to see. 'Stormy' means that there was rain and probably a lot of wind. 'Night' means that it isn't day. So, in other words, what I am reading means that it was a night that was really raining and blowing and it was hard to see."[23] It is not difficult to see why this long, tiresome process would frustrate anyone who badly wants to read but finds it a constant struggle to do so.

> " In the same way that reading is a cognitive, rather than associative, process for dyslexics, math is a cognitive process for those with dyscalculia. "

## Beyond Sloppy Penmanship

Many people who suffer from dyslexia also suffer from the writing disorder known as dysgraphia, but the two are not necessarily connected. In fact, people with dysgraphia may be good readers and excel at speaking verbally but struggle with spelling, have penmanship that no one can read, and be unable to transfer their thoughts into written form. Leane Somers, a reading specialist from New York, has a son who suffers from dysgraphia. She describes how she first discovered his learning disability and how he struggled with it in school:

> I knew my son had a problem with writing when I saw
> that his first-grade journal contained mostly drawings

and only a few sentences. In second grade, Austin was still reversing the letters *b* and *d*, something most of his peers had outgrown. His teachers called it laziness, but as he did his homework, I saw him labor to form letters correctly. He worked slowly, erased a lot, and cried.

Somers adds that dysgraphia makes the writing process "maddeningly slow, and the product often illegible. Forming letters requires such effort that a child may forget what he wanted to say in the first place."[24]

## When Math Seems Impossible

The learning disability dyscalculia is sometimes referred to as the "dyslexia of mathematics." In the same way that reading is a cognitive, rather than associative, process for dyslexics, math is a cognitive process for those with dyscalculia. Cimera uses the example of someone with normal math skills being asked, "Quick—what is 2 + 2?" and without giving it a second thought, he or she would know that the correct answer is 4. Solving the same problem for a person with dyscalculia, however, would be neither automatic nor simple, as Cimera explains: "Okay. 2 + 2. *Plus* means that it is an addition problem. That means that I am putting two numbers together. What are the two numbers? 2 and 2 . . . and 2 is 1 bigger than 1. Got it. So if I have one 2 and I were to add another 2, I would have . . . 1 . . . 2 . . . 3 . . . 4. The answer to 2 + 2 is 4."[25] Someone with dyscalculia faces many struggles because math is necessary for so many everyday activities such as shopping, paying for food in restaurants, reading and converting recipes for cooking, budgeting, balancing a checkbook, and even being able to read a traditional analog watch or clock.

## Day-to-Day Challenges

Learning disabilities can interfere with reading, writing, comprehension, communication, and solving mathematics problems. It is not uncommon for learning-disabled people to experience frustration, feelings of hopelessness, and an overall sense of failure. Fortunately, awareness has markedly grown over the past decades, and scientists know much more about learning disabilities today than they did in the past. Yet learning disabilities are still mysterious and unpredictable, and they make life a constant struggle for millions of men, women, and children.

# Primary Source Quotes*

# What Are Learning Disabilities?

> **Learning disabilities are real! Although they often aren't observed until a child is doing school-related tasks, a proven biological basis for LD exists, including emerging data that document genetic links for LD within families.**

—Sheldon Horowitz, "Ensuring School Success for Children with Learning Disabilities," *Children's Voice*, December 2005. www.cwla.org.

Horowitz is the director of professional services at the National Center for Learning Disabilities.

.................................................................................................................................................

> **The idea that a learning disability exists is a myth, a myth that has been established by an education system and government that is completely out of touch with what is happening in the classroom. . . . This myth is perpetuating illiteracy in our Western nations, who should know better.**

—Marta L. Marchisan, *Learning Disabilities: The Myth.* Bloomington, IN: AuthorHouse, 2005.

An educator for many years, Marchisan advocates on behalf of students whom she believes have been wrongly diagnosed as learning disabled.

.................................................................................................................................................

Bracketed quotes indicate conflicting positions.

* Editor's Note: While the definition of a primary source can be narrowly or broadly defined, for the purposes of Compact Research, a primary source consists of: 1) results of original research presented by an organization or researcher; 2) eyewitness accounts of events, personal experience, or work experience; 3) first-person editorials offering pundits' opinions; 4) government officials presenting political plans and/or policies; 5) representatives of organizations presenting testimony or policy.

Primary Source Quotes

**❝In general people with a learning disability/difference have the feeling that there is more in them; but in one way or another it won't come to the surface.❞**

—Jenny Burm, "The Consequences of Being Misunderstood and Receiving Labels," 2008. http://jennyburm.com.

Burm, who is dyslexic, seeks to help people with learning disabilities by contributing to greater understanding, respect, and tolerance.

---

**❝A child with a learning disability cannot try harder, pay closer attention, or improve motivation on their own; they need help to learn how to do those things.❞**

—Jeanne Segal et al., "Learning Disabilities: Types, Symptoms, and Interventions," HelpGuide, June 2008. www.helpguide.org.

Segal is a psychologist and managing editor of HelpGuide.

---

**❝Although a standard textbook definition does exist, there is considerable debate and little acceptance over what officially constitutes a learning disability, and this has led to over-identification and excessive labeling of students.❞**

—Marta L. Marchisan, *Learning Disabilities: The Myth*. Bloomington, IN: AuthorHouse, 2005.

An educator for many years, Marchisan advocates on behalf of students whom she believes have been wrongly diagnosed as learning disabled.

---

**❝Learning disabilities cannot be catalogued by race, gender, or religion.❞**

—Rebecca Fast, "Misunderstood Minds: Wasted Human Potential," speech, Equal Education Association of Nova Scotia, January 26, 2006. www.eeans.ca.

Fast was a student at Goshen College in Goshen, Indiana, when she gave her speech in the 2006 C. Henry Smith Peace Oratorical Contest.

---

**❝People with learning disabilities are often misunderstood. The mysteries of the mind aren't easily accepted these days, because people are quick to judge mental disabilities they don't understand, whereas a physical one is more acceptable.❞**

—Adam Brown, "Adult Autism Is Often Misunderstood," *Spartan Daily*, October 11, 2006. www.thespartandaily.com.

Brown is a graduate of South Carolina State University whose learning disability was caused by a form of autism known as Asperger's syndrome.

---

**❝About half of all kids with ADHD also have a specific learning disability. The most common problems are with reading (dyslexia) and handwriting.❞**

—Richard S. Kingsley (reviewer), "What Is ADHD?" *KidsHealth*, September 2008. http://kidshealth.org.

Kingsley is a child and adolescent psychiatrist at Alfred I. DuPont Hospital for Children in Wilmington, Delaware.

---

## What Are Learning Disabilities?

- According to the group Learning Disabilities Worldwide, up to **20 percent** of peope throughout the world suffer from learning disabilities.

- The National Center for Learning Disabilities states that **15 million** children, adolescents, and adults in the United States are affected by learning disabilities.

- According to the Centers for Disease Control and Prevention (CDC), in 2006, **4.7 million** children aged 3 to 17 had a learning disability.

- The National Center on Education Statistics states that **35 percent** of students enrolled in community colleges have learning disabilities.

- The CDC states that learning disabilities affect **10 percent** of boys aged 3 to 17 compared to **6 percent** of girls.

- The University of Michigan Health System states that **dyslexia** is the most common learning disability, affecting an estimated **80 percent** of students with learning disabilities.

- According to the International Dyslexia Association, as many as **20 percent** of the population has a language-based learning disability.

- A study by the University of California–Los Angeles showed that **3.3 percent** of college freshmen reported having a learning disability in 2008, compared with **0.5 percent** in 1983.

## Males More Likely to Be Diagnosed with Learning Disabilities

Many health-care professionals say that boys have learning disabilities at a much higher rate than girls, although this is controversial. Some argue that boys are just more likely to be diagnosed because they are more apt to exhibit disruptive behavior in the classroom. According to a February 2009 report by the Centers for Disease Control and Prevention, boys are nearly twice as likely as girls to be told they have a learning disability.

### Learning Disabilities Among Young People Aged 3 to 17 in the United States — 2007

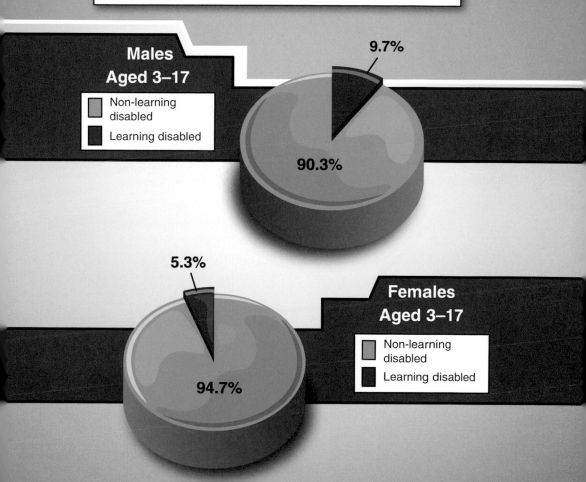

**Males Aged 3–17**

- Non-learning disabled
- Learning disabled

9.7%

90.3%

5.3%

**Females Aged 3–17**

- Non-learning disabled
- Learning disabled

94.7%

Source: Centers for Disease Control and Prevention, *Summary Health Statistics for U.S. Children: National Health Interview Survey, 2007*, January 2009. www.cdc.gov.

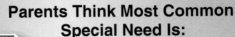

# Parents' Views on Special Needs

In a survey published in the November 2007 issue of *Exceptional Parent* magazine, nearly 1,000 parents shared their thoughts about the most common special needs based on personal experience with at least one special-needs child.

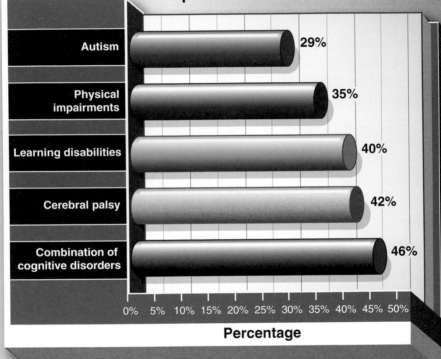

### Parents Think Most Common Special Need Is:

| | |
|---|---|
| Autism | 29% |
| Physical impairments | 35% |
| Learning disabilities | 40% |
| Cerebral palsy | 42% |
| Combination of cognitive disorders | 46% |

0%  5%  10%  15%  20%  25%  30%  35%  40%  45%  50%

**Percentage**

Note: Total exceeds 100 percent because participants were allowed to give more than one response.

Source: Deanna Tillisch, "New Research Provides a Snapshot of Parents with Children Who Have Special Needs," *Exceptional Parent*, November 2007, pp. 43–44.

- According to the National Institutes of Health, the prevalence of dyscalculia is **5 to 6 percent** among the school-aged population and is as common in girls as in boys.

## Students with Disabilities File the Most Complaints

Students with any type of disability, including learning disabilities, often suffer in school because their classmates ridicule them. During 2007 there were more complaints reported about disability-related discrimination than for any other reason.

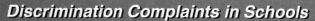

### Discrimination Complaints in Schools

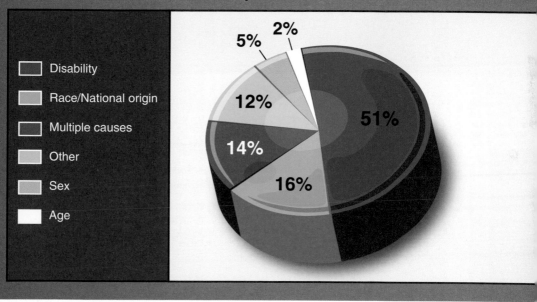

- Disability
- Race/National origin
- Multiple causes
- Other
- Sex
- Age

2%
5%
12%
14%
16%
51%

Source: U.S. Department of Education, "Performance and Accountability Report: Fiscal Year 2007," February 1, 2008. www.ed.gov.

- Students with learning disabilities often have **average or above-average intelligence**, and in some cases are **intellectually gifted**.

- A study published in March 2007 by the Learning Disabilities Association of Canada showed that **depression, anxiety**, and **unemployment** were significantly more common in people with learning disabilities than in those without.

# What Causes Learning Disabilities?

> **"There are many reasons why learning disability occurs. Impairments which cause or contribute to learning disability can happen before, during or after birth."**
>
> —British Institute of Learning Disabilities, an organization devoted to supporting people with learning disabilities in the United Kingdom.

> **"Currently, there are no known causes for learning disabilities."**
>
> —Jenifer Fox, educator, public speaker, and author.

Even though scientists have studied dyslexia, dyscalculia, and other learning disabilities for many years, no one has yet been able to pinpoint one distinct cause. Most agree, however, that something within the brains of learning-disabled people has gone awry, causing them to have difficulty receiving, processing, analyzing, and responding to information. Child and adolescent psychiatrist Larry B. Silver explains: "A learning disability is a neurological disorder. That is, it is the result of a nervous system that has been 'wired' a little differently. The brain is clearly not damaged, defective, or retarded. But, in certain areas, it processes information in a different way than it is supposed to."[26] In the past many researchers thought that learning disabilities might result from a single neurological problem, but now most suspect that the causes are much more complex. The prevailing scientific belief today is that several different areas of the brain could be affected by "faulty wiring," and the specific learning disabilities that individuals have depends on the particular area of the brain that is affected.

## The Intricacies of the Brain

In order to grasp the concept of a learning-disabled person's brain being wired differently, it is important to understand the brain and how it develops. Brain development begins when a human embryo is only about three weeks of age and no bigger than the head of a pin. At that stage the three primary sections of the brain form first: the forebrain, midbrain, and hindbrain. By the time the embryo is six weeks old, the largest and most complex part of the brain, the cerebrum, has formed, along with an outer layer known as the cerebral cortex, often referred to as "gray matter." The cortex is made up of specialized nerve cells known as neurons, which communicate with other neurons across connection points known as synapses. Neurons perform much like invisible fiber-optic cables that send and receive a constant stream of electrochemical signals. As brain development continues, neurons multiply at an unbelievably rapid rate and form complex networks with other areas of the brain. By the time the brain is fully formed, it contains billions and billions of neurons.

> " The prevailing scientific belief today is that several different areas of the brain could be affected by 'faulty wiring,' and the specific learning disabilities that individuals have depends on the particular area of the brain that is affected. "

The cerebral cortex is divided into four sections, or lobes, with each having its own specific functions. The frontal lobe is connected with problem solving, reasoning, memory, language, and decision making. The parietal lobe is associated with movement (motor skills), orientation, and processing sensory stimuli such as temperature, touch, and pain. The occipital lobe is associated with vision and color recognition, and the temporal lobe is involved with memory, emotion, hearing, and language. Although scientists do not know why, one or more of these areas may become miswired along the way, as the *Learning Disabilities Sourcebook* explains:

> Throughout pregnancy, this brain development is vulnerable to disruptions. If the disruption occurs early, the fetus may die, or the infant may be born with widespread disabilities and possibly mental retardation. If this disruption occurs later, when the cells are becoming specialized and moving into place, it may leave errors in the cell makeup, location, or connections. Some scientists believe that these errors may later show up as learning disorders.[27]

In the process of studying the human brain, scientists have linked several learning disabilities with particular areas of the cerebrum. In 2007 a team from the United Kingdom announced that they had identified the parietal lobe as the area of the brain where dyscalculia originates. Using transcranial magnetic stimulation, a procedure that uses magnetic fields to stimulate neurons, researchers temporarily disrupted neurons in the right parietal lobes of subjects who did not suffer from dyscalculia. Then the subjects were given a math test that involved comparing two digits, one larger in physical size than the other and the other larger numerically, such as two and four. Their ability to process numbers, as well as their reaction time, was markedly affected by the neuron disruption. Researcher Roi Cohen Kadosh explains what the discovery means: "This provides strong evidence that dyscalculia is caused by malformations in the right parietal lobe and provides solid grounds for further study on the physical abnormalities present in dyscalculics' brains."[28]

> " In the process of studying the human brain, scientists have linked several learning disabilities with particular areas of the cerebrum.

Also in 2007 researchers Sally E. and Bennett A. Shaywitz published their findings about the areas of the brain where dyslexia originates. They used functional magnetic resonance imaging to scan the brains of people with dyslexia as well as those who were not affected by it, and they could see a distinct difference in three separate areas within the left hemisphere: the frontal lobe, the parieto-temporal lobe (the area between the parietal and temporal lobes), and the occipito-temporal lobe (the area between the occipital and temporal lobes). This finding was significant because these areas are associated with word analysis or decoding, as well as the ability to read words fluently and automatically, which the Shaywitzes describe as "the hallmark of a skilled reader."[29]

## Family Ties

Even though the reason is not clearly understood, research has shown that learning disabilities tend to run in families. For instance, scientists have learned that as many as 50 percent of people with dyslexia have parents and/or siblings who also have reading problems. Although researchers have not found a single gene that is responsible for causing dyslexia, they have identified several "suspicious" genes that are likely connected in some way, and they continue to pursue genetic studies.

Dyscalculia has also been found to be hereditary. A study published in the January 2001 issue of *Journal of Learning Disabilities* showed that the familial prevalence of dyscalculia is nearly 10 times higher in families where one (or more) individuals suffered from the disorder than in the general population. From this the researchers concluded that genetics plays a significant role in whether someone develops the learning disability.

## Risks to the Fetus

When a baby is still in the womb, there are many natural factors in place (such as the amniotic fluid) that provide protection and allow development to progress. But the infant is at risk of being harmed if the mother engages in unhealthy behaviors. Scientists say that women who smoke, drink alcohol, or take drugs during pregnancy can harm their unborn child in many different ways, including causing damage to neurons, that could lead to learning disabilities. This risk exists because no matter what the mother ingests, it makes its way from her digestive system through the placenta and into the baby's bloodstream. In reference to alcoholic beverages, former surgeon general Richard Carmona states, "When a pregnant woman drinks alcohol, so does her baby."[30]

One of the most potentially dangerous risks to fetuses if pregnant women drink alcohol is known as fetal alcohol syndrome disorder (FASD). Babies born with FASD can suffer from a host of serious problems, including learning disabilities, as a February 2005 surgeon general advisory warned: "FASD is the full spectrum of birth defects caused by prenatal alcohol exposure. The spectrum may include mild and subtle changes, such as a slight learning disability and/or physical abnormality, through full-blown Fetal Alcohol Syndrome, which can include severe learning disabilities, growth deficiencies, abnormal facial features, and central nervous system disorders."[31]

Researchers have also studied the potential risk to fetuses if their mothers smoke marijuana during pregnancy. According to an April 2008 article in *Science Daily*, marijuana is among the most common illegal drugs to be used by women during childbearing years, "and there is growing concern that marijuana abuse during pregnancy, either alone or in combination with other drugs, may have serious effects on fetal brain development."[32] The article cites a study by a team of German scientists that involved injecting baby rats with different substances, including THC (the main psychoactive ingredient in marijuana) and alcohol. The team found that when the rats were given THC alone, it did not appear to cause nerve cell death. But when a combination of THC and alcohol was given, the nerve cell damage was particularly severe. From this the researchers concluded that THC increased the toxicity of alcohol, which could mean that women who smoke marijuana and drink alcohol are putting their babies at risk for neurological damage that could lead to learning disabilities and other problems. They also maintain that additional studies are warranted in order to further gauge the effects of marijuana on fetuses, as well as the potential risk when combined with alcohol.

> " Even though the reason is not clearly understood, research has shown that learning disabilities tend to run in families. "

## Heavy Metal Dangers

The fetus can also suffer neurological damage if the mother's blood contains high levels of mercury. Mercury is a heavy metal that occurs naturally in the earth's surface, but it is also released into the atmosphere by industrial operations such as mining and the burning of coal to generate electricity. When it is emitted into the air, it mixes with water vapor and then falls back to earth in the form of precipitation. It ends up in rivers, lakes, and oceans and is converted by microorganisms to the most toxic form: methylmercury, which has been shown to be especially prevalent in large predator fish such as sharks, tuna, king mackerel, and swordfish. The process begins when the methylmercury settles to the bottom of bodies of water and mixes with sediments, where it is eaten by microscopic organisms at the bottom of the food chain known as zooplankton. Small fish eat the zooplankton, larger fish eat the smaller fish, and at each stage, the mercury concentration in the fish increases. Thus, pregnant women who eat large amounts of fish, especially predator fish, are at risk of developing high mercury concentrations in own their bodies and then passing the toxins along to their babies. The result can be slow language development, memory deficiencies, short attention spans, and learning disabilities, among other problems.

> One of the most potentially dangerous risks to fetuses if pregnant women drink alcohol is known as fetal alcohol syndrome disorder (FASD).

Although the fetus is at risk for developing learning disabilities when environmental toxins are passed on from the mother, the hazard does not end at birth. Some children develop learning disabilities later if they have been exposed to heavy metals such as lead. Since 1978 lead-based paint has been outlawed in the United States, but it is still found in many older homes, especially those that were built before 1960. The Centers for Disease Control and Prevention states that lead paint remains in about 24 million housing units, and more than 300,000 children have elevated levels of lead in their blood. According to the Environmental Protection Agency, lead exposure causes language and behavior problems, nervous system damage, learning disabilities, and ADHD, among other ailments, and this continues to pose a significant risk to children in America.

High lead exposure often occurs when older homes with lead-based paint are renovated by contractors who use unsafe practices, such as burning paint off with open-flame torches. When such methods are used, the lead contained in the paint turns into a gas that becomes poisonous dust after it cools. The dust can collect on furniture, floors, and countertops, as well as linger in the air, and it is toxic to anyone who breathes it or ingests it. In 2003, after a contractor used an open-flame torch to burn the lead-based paint off the exterior of a house in Portland, Oregon, owner Tamara Rubin noticed what she describes as a "cloud" of dust that seeped inside the house—and not until later did she learn that the "cloud" she had observed was composed of lead. Almost immediately after the incident, Rubin's two sons developed what she believed to be the flu, but medical tests showed that both boys suffered from lead poisoning, "Now," she says, "my babies, who were fine before, have behavioral problems and long-term learning disabilities."[33] After Rubin learned that the contractor was not certified in lead-based paint removal, she sued him for damages and accepted a financial settlement. She now devotes her time to educating people about the hazards of lead-based paint.

> "Although the fetus is at risk for developing learning disabilities when environmental toxins are passed on from the mother, the hazard does not end at birth."

## Theories Galore

Many diseases and disorders have well-defined causes and can be prevented either by maintaining healthy lifestyles, taking medicine, or getting vaccinations. That is not the case, however, with learning disabilities. Scientists have identified many factors that are believed to contribute to learning disabilities, including damage to the developing brain, exposure to environmental toxins, and genetics. But just as learning disabilities are complex and mysterious, the same is true of their cause or causes, which are not well understood. As the National Association of Special Education Teachers explains: "Mental health professionals stress that since no one knows what causes learning disabilities, it doesn't help parents to look backward to search for possible reasons. There are too many possibilities to pin down the cause of the disability with certainty."[34]

# Primary Source Quotes*

# What Causes Learning Disabilities?

**66 LDs are not caused by environmental factors, like cultural differences, or bad teaching. 99**

—Kyla Boyse, "Learning Disabilities," University of Michigan Health System, June 2008. www.med.umich.edu.

Boyse is a registered nurse from Ann Arbor, Michigan.

**66 Learning problems can be the result of sensory problems, environmental or economic disadvantage. 99**

—Grafton, "Learning Disabilities." www.grafton.org.

Headquartered in Winchester, Virginia, Grafton provides health-care services to children and adults who suffer from a wide range of disabilities.

* Editor's Note: While the definition of a primary source can be narrowly or broadly defined, for the purposes of Compact Research, a primary source consists of: 1) results of original research presented by an organization or researcher; 2) eyewitness accounts of events, personal experience, or work experience; 3) first-person editorials offering pundits' opinions; 4) government officials presenting political plans and/or policies; 5) representatives of organizations presenting testimony or policy.

Primary Source Quotes

66 Learning disabilities are caused by a difference in brain structure that is present at birth and is often hereditary. They affect the way the brain processes information. This processing is the main function involved in learning. 99

—National Institute of Child Health and Human Development, "Learning Disabilities," February 23, 2007. www.nichd.nih.gov.

The National Institute of Child Health and Human Development conducts and supports research on topics related to the health of children, adults, families, and populations.

66 Just as our blue eyes, dark hair, or height can be inherited, a number of researchers have established that reading disorders seem to be passed from generation to generation. 99

—Joan M. Harwell and Rebecca Williams Jackson, *The Complete Learning Disabilities Handbook*. San Francisco: Wiley, 2008.

Harwell and Jackson are educators who specialize in learning disabilities.

66 New developments in neuroscience and brain imaging now reveal that learning disabilities are not a fad, not an excuse, not a reflection of baby boomers' obsession with their children—but the result of brain wiring that is different from typical brains. 99

—Laura Schenone, "An 'A' That's Not a Scarlet Letter," Nonverbal Learning Disorders Association, July 7, 2006. www.nlda.org.

Schenone is an author whose son has several learning disabilities.

66 Learning disabilities seem to be caused by the brain, but the exact causes are not yet known. They tend to run in families. 99

—C.S. Mott Children's Hospital, "Learning Disabilities." http://med.umich.edu.

The C.S. Mott Children's Hospital is part of the University of Michigan Health System.

**66** No one's exactly sure what causes learning disabilities. But researchers do have some theories as to why they develop.**99**

—D'Arcy Lyness, "Learning Disabilities," TeensHealth, March 2007. http://kidshealth.org.

Lyness is a child and adolescent psychologist from Wayne, Pennsylvania.

................................................................................................................................................

**66** Injuries before birth or in early childhood probably account for some later learning problems. Children born prematurely and children who had medical problems soon after birth sometimes have learning disabilities.**99**

—Bob Myers, "About Learning Disabilities," HealthyPlace, December 20, 2008. www.healthyplace.com.

Myers is a child psychologist from California.

................................................................................................................................................

# What Causes Learning Disabilities?

- According to the National Center for Learning Disabilities, there is often **no apparent cause** for a learning disability.

- Risk factors for learning disabilities include **genetics, stress during pregnancy, birth trauma, and/or incidents after birth** such as head injuries, poor nutrition, or exposure to toxic substances.

- Children whose mothers **smoked**, regularly **drank alcohol**, or **took drugs** during pregnancy are at a **higher risk** of developing learning disabilities than those whose mothers had healthy pregnancies.

- A study published in 2009 showed that pregnant women who had just a few episodes of **drinking four or more alcoholic beverages a day** increased the risk of their child developing mental health problems, including learning disabilities.

- According to the Centers for Disease Control and Prevention (CDC), children with fair or poor health are **five times as likely** as those with excellent or very good health to suffer from learning disabilities.

- The CDC states that children of families with annual income of less than **$20,000** have learning disabilities twice as often as children of families whose income is **$75,000** or more.

- Family history is one of the major risk factors for dyslexia; **23 to 65 percent** of children diagnosed with the disorder have a parent who also has it.

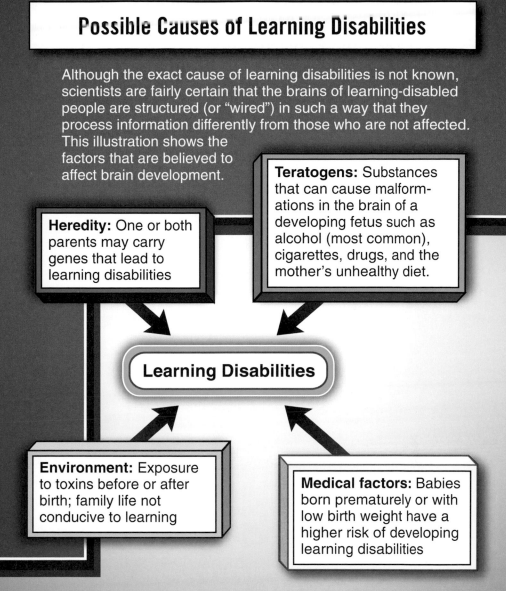

## Possible Causes of Learning Disabilities

Although the exact cause of learning disabilities is not known, scientists are fairly certain that the brains of learning-disabled people are structured (or "wired") in such a way that they process information differently from those who are not affected. This illustration shows the factors that are believed to affect brain development.

**Heredity:** One or both parents may carry genes that lead to learning disabilities

**Teratogens:** Substances that can cause malformations in the brain of a developing fetus such as alcohol (most common), cigarettes, drugs, and the mother's unhealthy diet.

**Learning Disabilities**

**Environment:** Exposure to toxins before or after birth; family life not conducive to learning

**Medical factors:** Babies born prematurely or with low birth weight have a higher risk of developing learning disabilities

Source: Robert Evert Cimera, *Learning Disabilities: What Are They?* Lanham, MD: Rowman & Littlefield, 2007.

- The CDC states that among children aged 6 to 17, the incidence of learning disabilities is markedly higher among those who live in a **mother-only family** than among those living in a **two-parent family**.

## Learning Disabilities Highest Among Low-Income Children

Most scientists insist that learning disabilities are not directly related to socioeconomic status because learning-disabled children come from all walks of life. But according to a July 2008 report by the Centers for Disease Control and Prevention, the frequency is highest among lower-income families and lowest among the highest-income families.

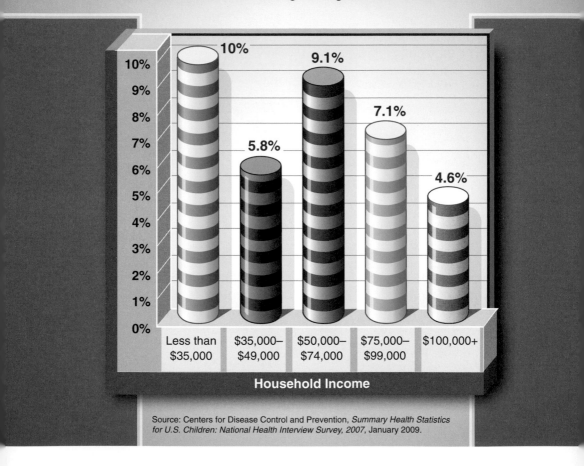

Source: Centers for Disease Control and Prevention, *Summary Health Statistics for U.S. Children: National Health Interview Survey, 2007,* January 2009.

- In 2007 at least **10 million** children's items were recalled because they contained **lead**, which has been linked to brain damage and learning disabilities.

# The Mercury Connection

Mercury occurs naturally in the environment, but huge amounts of the toxic substance are emitted into the atmosphere by coal-fired power plants and other industrial sources. According to the U.S. Environmental Protection Agency (EPA), the most common way people are exposed to mercury is by eating fish, especially large predatory fish such as sharks, tuna, king mackerel, and swordfish. The EPA warns that pregnant women with high levels of mercury in their bodies can pass it along to their unborn children through the placenta, or pass it to infants through breast milk, and this may contribute toward learning disabilities and other birth defects. This illustration shows how mercury in the atmosphere ends up in the environment and works its way through the food chain.

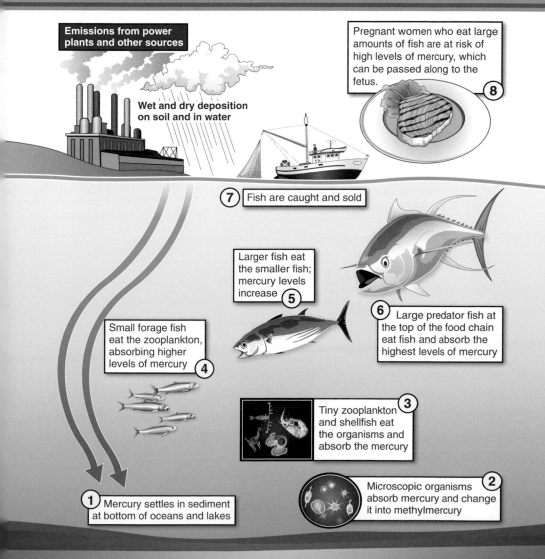

Emissions from power plants and other sources

Wet and dry deposition on soil and in water

Pregnant women who eat large amounts of fish are at risk of high levels of mercury, which can be passed along to the fetus. 8

7 Fish are caught and sold

Larger fish eat the smaller fish; mercury levels increase 5

6 Large predator fish at the top of the food chain eat fish and absorb the highest levels of mercury

Small forage fish eat the zooplankton, absorbing higher levels of mercury 4

Tiny zooplankton and shellfish eat the organisms and absorb the mercury 3

Microscopic organisms absorb mercury and change it into methylmercury 2

1 Mercury settles in sediment at bottom of oceans and lakes

# Learning Disabilities and Low Birth Weight

Studies have shown that attention deficit hyperactivity disorder (ADHD) and learning disabilities (LD) are more prevalent among children who were born with a lower than average birth weight. This study was included in a July 2008 report by the Centers for Disease Control and Prevention.

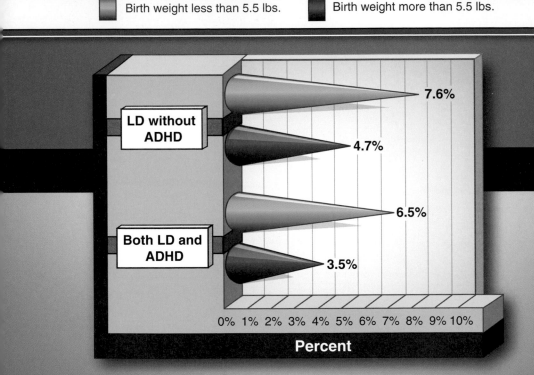

Birth weight less than 5.5 lbs.    Birth weight more than 5.5 lbs.

LD without ADHD — 7.6%

LD without ADHD — 4.7%

Both LD and ADHD — 6.5%

Both LD and ADHD — 3.5%

0% 1% 2% 3% 4% 5% 6% 7% 8% 9% 10%

**Percent**

Source: Patricia N. Pastor and Cynthia A. Reuben, "Diagnosed Attention Deficit Hyperactivity Disorder and Learning Disability, United States, 2004–2006," Centers for Disease Control and Prevention, July 2008. www.cdc.gov.

- A genetic condition known as **fragile X syndrome** is the most commonly inherited cause of mental impairment, including learning disabilities.

# Can People Overcome Learning Disabilities?

66 **Most people with learning disabilities learn to adapt to their learning differences, and they learn strategies that help them accomplish their goals and dreams.** 99

—D'Arcy Lyness, a child and adolescent psychologist from Wayne, Pennsylvania.

66 **The struggle to become independent remains difficult for people with learning disabilities.** 99

—Dale S. Brown, author and learning disabilities advocate.

W hen Aubrey Goodell was a toddler, she was an intelligent, so-cial child as well as emotionally mature for her age. Talking was difficult for her, however, and she often exhibited outbursts of anger. Once she started school she made little progress, and by the time she was in the third grade, she still could not read or write. Her anger was also causing her problems, as she explains: "You don't know why you can't understand and why other kids don't like you. You just know you're angry, so you yell and throw things."[35] Goodell was tested and found to have a learning disability that involved short-term memory problems and difficulty processing information. She was placed in remedial classes, which made her feel even worse about herself than she already did, and she continued to fall behind in school.

Goodell's mother was determined that her daughter would succeed.

Over the following years the girl attended 10 different schools and finally found one that emphasized her strengths and what she *could* do, rather than focusing on what she could *not* do. Her progress was slow at first, but she gradually began to show significant improvement in her schoolwork. She learned to prioritize and organize her work, used books on tape instead of print versions, and worked with her teachers to restructure written assignments. Today, at the age of 17, Goodell is doing well in most of her academic subjects. Although reading and writing are still challenging for her, and she has to study as much as six hours per night, she is a happy, optimistic, and confident young woman who plans to go to college. Her mother says she has made "remarkable progress," and adds that her daughter has learned skills that will benefit her for the rest of her life. "She expects to work hard, and expects life to come with conflict and compromise. She knows her destiny is in her hands."[36]

> " Psychologists and other health professionals say that in order for children to overcome learning disabilities, ongoing support from parents and educators is crucial. "

## The Perils of Labeling

Psychologists and other health professionals say that in order for children to overcome learning disabilities, ongoing support from parents and educators is crucial. In their book *The Mislabeled Child*, learning specialists and physicians Brock and Fernette Eide explain that the most important help for children with learning challenges is having mentors who believe in them unconditionally and have faith in them. They write:

> Even children who face serious learning challenges can grow up to lead successful and satisfying lives if they are encouraged to develop their strengths, overcome their weaknesses, and maintain a clear and confident vision of their own eventual success. A child's ego is seldom strong enough to withstand constant negative feedback

at school, unless she receives even stronger messages of optimism and hope from someone she loves and respects. Keeping alive a child's positive vision of herself and her future should be the number-one goal of parents, teachers, and adult mentors.[37]

The Eides share the experience of a boy named Michael who was highly intelligent and achieved mostly As in elementary school, but who began a downward slide in the fifth grade. He could not keep up with the growing demands for reading and writing in class, and he constantly felt overwhelmed and depressed, often referring to himself as stupid or dumb and hitting himself as punishment. He grew to hate school and often complained of headaches or stomachaches so he could stay home.

Michael's parents ached for their son and wanted desperately to help him. When they met with the school district, however, they were told that he could not have a learning problem because his test scores were average or above-average. School officials explained that either Michael was not applying himself or perhaps had unrealistic expectations for his academic progress—in other words, maybe he was just not capable of achieving as much as he thought he should. Michael's parents were angry over this arbitrary labeling of their son, and they refused to accept that he was lazy, not trying, or not smart enough to keep up with his classmates.

> " In many cases students struggle not just because of their own [learning] disabilities, but because the environment is not a good fit for them. "

After independent testing showed that Michael's IQ was nearly 140 (close to the genius level), his parents consulted with the Eides, who performed a number of tests and determined that he was dyslexic. They write:

> His struggles in school were caused not only by the brain-based learning challenges that made it hard for him to read, write, spell, and move in a coordinated fashion, but also by the fact that he was a *mislabeled child*. Michael was neither lazy nor careless nor slow. Michael had dyslexia.

Because he was mislabeled, his learning challenges were neither clearly understood nor properly addressed.[38]

Once Michael's learning disability was identified, his parents had a better understanding of what needed to be done to help him overcome it. They had renewed confidence that their son would be able to learn and succeed in school as well as in life and live up to his full potential—no longer would Michael view himself as someone who was stupid, dumb, or doomed to fail.

## Specialized Education

Children who are learning disabled often make excellent progress in school if teaching is tailored to their unique needs. But in many cases students struggle not just because of their own disabilities, but because the environment is not a good fit for them. Educator and author Jenifer Fox explains: "We seldom discuss the possibility that learning problems have their roots in a variety of places other than in the child's brain. We don't hear about a 'teaching disability,' a 'parenting disability,' a 'school disability,' or a 'federal policy disability.'" Fox adds that a curriculum that works for nonimpaired students may not be at all effective for those with learning disabilities, and this can impede their progress and add to their learning struggles. "Somewhere along the line," she writes, "it was determined that if students don't perform at a high level in all content areas, the areas in which their performance is weak should deem them to be considered disabled. Somewhere along the line it was determined that success means that every student be perfectly well rounded in all subject areas."[39]

> **Even with legislation in place that mandates specialized education for students who are learning disabled, many young people still slip through the cracks.**

According to Fox, the schools that are most successful at helping students overcome their learning disabilities are those that are willing to discard traditional methods of teaching and create customized programs that "meet students where they are and take them where they have faith they can go."[40] In this way young people build on their strengths and learn strategies for working with—and overcoming—their weaknesses.

Don Johnston is also convinced that schools must meet the unique, individual needs of learning-disabled students. Now a successful business owner in Volo, Illinois, Johnston struggled for many years with reading, and his teachers were not always supportive; in fact, some demeaned him in front of his classmates. One day a teacher wrote the letters $H - O - W$ on the blackboard and then turned to Johnston and asked

> **Many people with learning disabilities who struggle through-out elementary, middle, and high school go on to college and make exceptional progress.**

him what she had spelled. He writes: "I stared at the word. I had no idea. 'Pay attention, Don,' Mrs. Arns yelled. 'You are so lazy!'"[41] Johnston's learning problems continued to plague him, and he was not able to read until the ninth grade. Then, due to the support of several devoted teachers, along with his own determination to succeed, things began to turn around for him. Johnston graduated from high school, went on to college, and earned both bachelor's and master's degrees.

Because of the many challenges he overcame, Johnston wanted to do something to help others who face similar struggles, so he founded a company that develops technologies, tools, and instructional materials to improve the skills of people with reading and writing difficulties. "Our educational system changes," he writes, "when we stop looking at students as a problem that needs to be fixed and start looking at how we can differentiate instruction and find creative ways to adapt our teaching to the unique needs of our students."[42]

## Wasted Years

Even with legislation in place that mandates specialized education for students who are learning disabled, many young people still slip through the cracks. Their problems may go undiagnosed or be misdiagnosed, either of which can result in years of frustration and lost opportunities.

This was the case with Jarron Draper, who attended school in Atlanta, Georgia, beginning in the second grade. At the age of 7 he could not read, was writing at kindergarten level, and did not know the sounds of the alphabet. Upon the recommendation of his teachers, Draper was tested by his school in 1998 and diagnosed as mentally retarded. He was placed in special education classes and over the following years made little or no academic progress. By the time he was 16 years old and in the ninth grade, Draper's math and reading levels were still only at the third-grade level, and his spelling was at the second-grade level. Because he was doing so poorly, his family requested that the school provide him with private, one-on-one tutoring in order to close the achievement gap in his studies. The school would not honor this request, however, and Draper's academic progress continued to deteriorate.

> "Today there are specialized education and therapy programs that are tailored to people's individual needs and that can help them compensate for their learning problems and become successful in life."

In 2004 a psychologist evaluated Draper and found that there were marked discrepancies between his intellectual potential and his academic skills—the hallmark of a learning disability. She determined that he suffered from dyslexia and recommended that he begin receiving intensive schooling specially designed for his unique needs. After the school did not comply with the recommendation, Draper's family filed a formal complaint with the court. At a hearing before an administrative law judge, Draper's attorney argued that the school system had neglected the young man's educational needs for years and that he deserved to be compensated for that. The judge ruled in favor of Draper and his family and required Atlanta Public Schools to pay up to $152,000 so he could attend a private school for four years and get the specialized help that had long been denied him.

Many people with learning disabilities who struggle throughout elementary, middle, and high school go on to college and make exceptional progress. One example is Lindsey Disher, who as a high school freshman had a difficult time understanding the scientific concepts in her biology textbook even if she read the same material over and over. Fortunately, an observant English teacher noticed that Disher often inverted and reversed letters in her handwritten assignments, and she suggested that the girl be tested for a learning disability. The test revealed that Disher had dyslexia, which explained her ongoing struggles with reading and writing—but Disher also learned what the diagnosis did *not* mean, as she explains: "Just because you have a learning disability doesn't mean you are not as smart or you can't excel or do what you want to in your education. It just means you learn differently."[43]

Disher began to make amazing progress, finishing high school in just three years. By the age of 19, she had completed two years of college, earning As and Bs in her classes. She says that she has also learned to be more self-confident, which has enabled her to study better for tests, not be afraid to speak out in class, "and to genuinely know that I can go as far in the academic setting as those around me."[44]

To meet the needs of learning-disabled students, some colleges have implemented specialized programs. At the University of Arizona, for instance, the Strategic Alternative Learning Center provides special-needs students with tutoring; access to computer, mathematics, and writing labs; and the services of a learning specialist. A similar program is at Marshall University in Huntington, West Virginia, where learning-disabled students may participate in Higher Education for Learning Problems (HELP). Of the roughly 200 students involved with the HELP program during 2007, 50 achieved high enough grades to make the dean's list.

## Everyone Has Potential

Much progress has been made over the years in developing ways to help people overcome learning disabilities. Today there are specialized education and therapy programs that are tailored to individual needs that can help those who are learning-disabled compensate for their problems and become successful in life. Yet numerous challenges still exist. Even now, parents and educators often do not recognize the signs of learning disabilities, assuming that children are at fault by not paying attention, applying themselves, or studying hard enough. In order for people to overcome their learning disabilities, as so many already have, these misconceptions need to change.

# Primary Source Quotes*

## Can People Overcome Learning Disabilities?

66 **Although the world is full of suffering, it is full also of the overcoming of it.**99

—Helen Keller, *The World I Live In*. New York: Century, 1908.

Blind and deaf since she was a toddler, Keller overcame her disabilities and became a world-famous author.

66 **Technically speaking, it is possible for a student to have a learning disability, be taught how to learn more effectively, thus overcome the inability to receive an appropriate education, and therefore no longer have a learning disability.**99

—Robert Evert Cimera, *Learning Disabilities: What Are They?* Lanham, MD: Rowman & Littlefield, 2007.

Cimera is an associate professor in the Department of Special Education at Kent State University in Ohio.

* Editor's Note: While the definition of a primary source can be narrowly or broadly defined, for the purposes of Compact Research, a primary source consists of: 1) results of original research presented by an organization or researcher; 2) eyewitness accounts of events, personal experience, or work experience; 3) first-person editorials offering pundits' opinions; 4) government officials presenting political plans and/or policies; 5) representatives of organizations presenting testimony or policy.

**❝Students with learning disabilities often develop unique ways of learning effectively, yet they share the frustration of coping with a disability that is virtually 'invisible' and often misunderstood.❞**

> —York University, *Faculty Resource Guide: Teaching Students with Disabilities*, 2007. www.yorku.ca.

York, located in Toronto, is Canada's third-largest university.

........................................................................................................................

**❝When I became a mother, my youngest daughter was diagnosed with dyslexia in second grade. . . . Now grown, my daughter is happy and successful, and loves to read! It took parental support, tutoring (from 2nd to 9th grade), and her own hard work, but she did it.❞**

> —Diane Peters Mayer, "Dyslexia Is Not Destiny," Overcoming School Anxiety Blog, December 13, 2008. http://overcomingschoolanxiety.com.

Mayer is a psychotherapist who works with children, adolescents, adults, and couples.

........................................................................................................................

**❝Bruce Jenner, Olympic decathlon champion, barely got through school. He was diagnosed with dyslexia and found that through sports he could hold his head up with friends and feel good about himself.❞**

> —Bernadette Angle, "Winning the 'Game' Against Learning Disabilities," *Coach and Athletic Director*, September 2007.

Angle is a professor at Youngstown State University in Youngstown, Ohio.

........................................................................................................................

**❝Over the years I have coped with my reading disability to the point that I don't have many problems processing information anymore, but there are times when I have to read over and over because it doesn't make sense, and then I realize that I read it wrong. The sentence didn't say what I thought it did.❞**

> —Charlene Collins, "Tools to Help Kids with Learning Disabilities," Associated Content, October 21, 2008. www.associatedcontent.com.

Collins is a writer from the United Kingdom who has dyslexia.

........................................................................................................................

66 For many with learning disabilities, the early patterns of failure are so relentless and disheartening that they head down self-destructive paths. Studies have shown increased rates of arrests, divorces and job-hopping, for instance. 99

—Kathy Bergen, "How 4 People Turned Learning Disabilities into Stories of Success, Fortune and Happiness," *Chicago Tribune*, April 9, 2006. www.allkindsofminds.org.

Bergen is a staff reporter with the *Chicago Tribune*.

66 Currently, there are tens of thousands of individuals with [learning disabilities] in the workforce, some of whom are doing remarkably well, some of whom are struggling. 99

—Paul J. Gerber, "Understanding Adults with Learning Disabilities," *Journal of Employee Assistance*, January 2008.

Gerber is a professor at Virginia Commonwealth University.

66 If a student is underperforming or not learning, subjecting him or her to more of the same, perhaps louder or for longer periods of time, will not achieve a different result. This is a punitive approach to teaching that increases student alienation. 99

—Gary Stager, "Stop the Insanity," *District Administration*, October 2007.

Stager is senior editor of *District Administration* and editor of the *Pulse: Education's Place for Debate*.

66 While at times the classroom may be a place of avoidance and isolation, the field or gym may serve as the environment in which an individual with learning disabilities shines. 99

—Bernadette Angle, "Winning the 'Game' Against Learning Disabilities," *Coach and Athletic Director*, September 2007.

Angle is a professor at Youngstown State University in Youngstown, Ohio.

# Can People Overcome Learning Disabilities?

- Under the Individuals with Disabilities Education Act (IDEA) and Americans with Disabilities Act, people with learning disabilities of all ages are **protected against discrimination** and are **entitled to accommodations** in the classroom and workplace.

- According to the Mayo Clinic, children with **severe dyslexia** may never be able to read well and may need training for jobs that do not require strong reading skills.

- The U.S. Department of Education states that during the 2006–2007 school year, nearly **7 million** youth aged 3 to 21 received special education under IDEA.

- Of the students who were served under IDEA in 2006–2007, **1 percent** were American Indian/Alaska Native, **2 percent** were Asian/Pacific Islander, **17 percent** were Hispanic, **20 percent** were black, and **59 percent** were white.

- Since 1980 a larger percentage of children and youth aged 3 to 21 have received **special education services for learning disabilities** than for any other types of disabilities.

- More than **33 percent** of students with learning disabilities drop out of high school, which is twice the rate of students who are not learning disabled.

# Learning-Disabled People Who Beat the Odds

After struggling with learning disabilities for most of their lives, many people have overcome them and achieved levels of success that they once believed were impossible. Here are some of the most well known.

| Name | Achievements |
| --- | --- |
| Billy Blanks | Martial artist, actor, and creator of Tai-Bo |
| Erin Brockovich | Director of environmental research at the Masry and Vititoe law offices whose real-life experience inspired the movie named after her |
| Delow Cosgrove | Cardiothoracic surgeon and CEO of the Cleveland Clinic |
| Whoopi Goldberg | Actress and comedienne |
| Tommy Hilfiger | Internationaly known fashion designer |
| Jack Horner | Paleontologist and consultant to director Steven Spielberg on the movies *Jurassic Park* and *The Lost World* |
| Jewel | Pop music singer |
| Don Johnston | Educator, author, business owner, and advocate for those with learning disabilities |
| Dexter Scott King | Son of the late Martin Luther King Jr. and president of the Atlanta-based Martin Luther King Jr. Center for Non-Violent Social Change |
| Jay Leno | Comedian |
| Gavin Newsom | Mayor of San Francisco |
| Paul Orfalea | Founder of Kinko's |
| Nelson Rockefeller | Former governor of New York and vice president of the United States under Gerald Ford |
| Richard Rogers | One of the most respected architects in Great Britain |
| Charles Schwab | CEO of the largest brokerage firm in the United States, Charles Schwab Corporation |
| Vince Vaughn | Actor who starred in the movies *Starsky and Hutch*, *Jurassic Park II*, and *Wedding Crashers* |

Source: Great Schools, "Famous People with Dyslexia, Other LD, and/or AD/HD," August 2008. www.greatschools.net.

## Employment of Disabled Versus Nondisabled Americans

The Americans with Disabilities Act (ADA) defines disability as "a physical or mental impairment that substantially limits one or more of the major life activities of an individual." Learning is included as a "major life activity." Under the ADA, businesses and government employers cannot legally discriminate against qualified applicants or employees on the basis of disabilities—yet the employment rate for disabled people is substantially lower than that of nondisabled people.

### Employment Status of the Civilian Population for People Aged 16 and Older

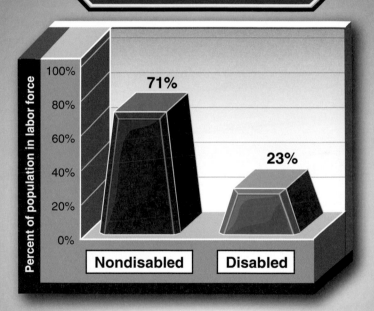

Sources: U.S. Department of Justice, "ADA Home Page," April 6, 2009. www.ada.gov; U.S. Bureau of Labor Statistics, "New Monthly Data Series on the Employment Status of People with a Disability," April 3, 2009. www.bls.gov.

- The Learning Disability Institute states that previously undetected learning disabilities have been diagnosed in **50 percent** of juvenile delinquents.

- According to the Center for Sex Offender Management, **30 to 60 percent** of juvenile sex offenders suffer from learning disabilities.

- The Mayo Clinic states that if dyslexia is left untreated, it can lead to **behavioral problems**, delinquency, aggression, and withdrawal or alienation from friends, parents, and teachers.

- According to a study published in March 2008 by the National Center for Special Education Research, young adults with learning disabilities are more likely than those in many other disability categories to report **smoking, drinking, and marijuana** use.

- A study published in the July 1, 2008, issue of the *Journal of Learning Disabilities* showed that the **rate of employment** and **amount of earned income** of learning-disabled young adults ages 21 to 24 were not significantly lower than those of their peers who did not have learning disabilities.

# Can Learning Disabilities Be Cured?

**❝There is no 'cure' for learning disabilities. They are life-long. However, children with LD can be high achievers and can be taught ways to get around the learning disability.❞**

> —National Dissemination Center for Children with Disabilities, which provides information on child and youth disabilities, programs and services, special education laws, and effective practices for children with disabilities.

**❝I have recently learned that learning disabilities are forever. You don't 'grow out of it.' It appears that dyslexia has, and will continue to be, my constant companion.❞**

> —Taylor Beattie, a former Green Beret with the U.S. Army.

Medical science has produced amazing achievements over the years in preventing and curing diseases. It is now known, for example, that healthy lifestyle choices can prevent many cases of heart disease, diabetes, and cancer. Vaccinations prevent deadly illnesses such as polio, influenza, and tetanus, and antibiotics cure numerous bacterial infections that in the past resulted in certain death. But unlike any of these physical ailments, there is not a surefire way of preventing learning disabilities, nor is there a cure. Most scientists say that even though people can and do overcome them, learning disabilities last for a lifetime. One of the highest priorities for researchers today is to identify what causes

65

learning disabilities, because descriptions such as "thought to be caused by" or "likely contributes to" are vague and insufficient. Scientists were not able to develop vaccines for polio or influenza until they isolated the viruses that cause the diseases, nor could they create antibiotics to cure infections without fully understanding how the infections occurred in the first place. The same is true of learning disabilities. Until more is known about the cause, a cure will remain elusive.

## Secrets Within the Brain

Because learning disabilities are widely believed to be associated with faulty brain wiring, many current studies are focused on brain research. With each new study scientists learn more about the brain and its functions, which brings them closer to determining the cause and finding a cure. In October 2008 a team of scientists from the University of California–Los Angeles released the findings of a study that traced learning disabilities to an imbalance in signals that increase and decrease neural activity in the brain. The National Institute of Mental Health (NIMH), which helped fund the research, explains: "Just as traffic signals enable safe traversing of the roadways, so too does the brain's machinery for learning and memory rely on its own stop-and-go signals."[45]

> With each new study scientists learn more about the brain and its functions, which brings them closer to determining the cause and finding a cure.

During a previous study with genetically altered mice, the researchers found that a gene known as NF-1 was responsible for causing memory impairment in many people who suffered from the genetic disorder neurofibromatosis. "The researchers traced the deficit to disrupted regulation in a web of intracellular traffic signals controlling a process that strengthens the connections between nerve cells—the stuff of memory," writes the NIMH. "Yet, exactly how the signal disruption interferes with this process remained unclear."[46]

The 2008 study solved the mystery. The team discovered that the cause of the disrupted memory signals was an increased release of a chemical neurotransmitter called GABA, which the NIMH says is the "brain's equivalent of a red light. Too much GABA puts the brakes on a neuron's ability to change and strengthen its connections—the critical requirement for learning and memory."[47]

Once the scientists had determined the root of the memory impairment, they used a GABA-blocking drug to treat the mice—and the creatures' memory performance markedly improved. From this the scientists concluded that the right balance of GABA in the brain is necessary for optimal learning and memory, and that at least some types of learning disabilities may be reversed if this balance is achieved. This was an exciting finding, although it will likely be years before GABA-blocking drugs are used to treat humans, as lead scientist Alcino Silva explains: "It won't be a single step from the mechanism to finding a drug." Silva says that as with other complex diseases and disorders, it takes a long time for scientific discoveries to become actual medical applications. But, he adds, "the more insight we have into the mechanisms responsible, the more likely it is that our treatment efforts will be effective. . . . We are at the beginning of a wonderful journey into how the human mind works. We are developing a highly detailed view of what goes on in the brain when we learn and remember. There is nothing more inspiring; it's what makes us who we are."[48]

> " In February 2009 a team of Canadian scientists announced the findings of a long-term research project that linked a particular brain protein with learning disabilities. "

## A Learning Disability Cure?

In February 2009 a team of Canadian scientists announced the findings of a long-term research project that linked a particular brain protein with learning disabilities. The protein, known as Neto1, is crucial for neurons within the hippocampus (the primary part of the brain involved in memory and learning) to be able to talk to each other. If the protein is missing or dysfunctional, normal neural communication is inhibited, which can result in learning impairments. Using two groups of mice, one that had been genetically altered to be missing the gene and another group of wild mice that had not, the scientists performed an experiment to test the creatures' cognitive functions and measure their ability to learn new skills. They put the mice in water and made them swim through a maze in order to find a hidden safety platform that would enable them to climb out. The mice without Neto1 continuously got lost and were not able to find the platform, whereas the unaltered mice found it every time, locating it faster with each try.

> **When the mouse brains were examined under a fluorescent microscope, neurons and neural connections glowed in a riot of colors, much like a rainbow.**

The researchers concluded that since they had identified a specific protein deficiency, there was great potential for the condition to be corrected. They gave the learning-disabled mice drugs known as ampakines, which are currently being tested with patients who suffer from Alzheimer's disease. The difference was apparent almost immediately, with the genetically altered mice performing the tests as well as the wild mice. Roderick McInnes, one of the lead scientists in the research project, says that the implications of this study are profound because the discovery could eventually lead to a cure for learning disorders. He explains: "Neurologists and neuroscientists have always tended to think that if the brain is abnormal at birth, nothing can be done to improve intellectual function, and that special education was virtually the only assistance available. It is no longer a fantasy to think that drug treatment might, in the future, be available for such patients."[49]

## The Brainbow

Brain studies are challenging because neurons are densely packed and neural activity is not easy for scientists to observe. In October 2007 a team from Harvard University developed a sophisticated brain imaging technique called the Brainbow, which allows them to trace neural connections to gain a better understanding of the brain's organization and function. The researchers removed genes from coral and jellyfish, both of which contain pigments that cause colors to form. After bundling the pigment-inducing genes into microscopic packages of deoxyribonucleic acid (DNA), the researchers inserted the genes into the brains of mice. The creatures had been genetically altered to contain a bacteria gene known as Cre, which activates the color genes inside brain cells. When the mouse brains were examined under a fluorescent microscope, neurons and neural connections glowed in a riot of colors, much like a rainbow—hence the name.

An article in LiveScience describes the images as resembling abstract color paintings, which are "both beautiful and informative. They look like they could hang in a modern art museum and are among the most detailed images of neuronal connections ever made."[50] Although Brainbow technology has only been used in experiments with mice, researchers believe that it holds tremendous potential for studying human disorders such as autism, mental retardation, and learning disabilities, all of which are related in some way to brain deficiencies.

## Can Brains Be Rewired?

The human brain is a fascinating, complex organ about which much is yet to be discovered. Researchers know that brains have an intricate wiring system that enables humans to move, think, talk, laugh, cry—all bodily functions in one way or another connect back to the brain. Why the brain of someone with a learning disability is wired differently is not known. But many scientists wonder, would it be possible to correct that deficiency by changing the way a brain is wired? According to a study published in August 2008, in some people that may indeed be possible. Researchers from Carnegie Mellon's Center for Cognitive Brain Imaging (CCBI) used functional magnetic resonance imaging (fMRI) technology to scan the brains of 22 fifth-grade students with dyslexia, as well as a control group of 23 non-dyslexic readers. The scans focused on measuring blood flow through

> " Follow-up scans showed that the differences between the dyslexic children and those in the control group had all but vanished. "

the different parts of the brain as the children were reading aloud. Preliminary scans showed that in the dyslexic children, there was significantly less activity in a number of regions in the parieto-temporal area than in the same area in the brains of control group members.

After the scans had been performed, the dyslexic children received 100 hours of remedial reading with teachers and then immediately underwent a second round of fMRI scans. The researchers could clearly see that that their parieto-temporal regions were much closer to normal—but the most exciting finding was discovered a year later. Follow-up scans showed that the differences between the dyslexic children and those in the control group had all but vanished. CCBI director Marcel Just refers to this as neuroplasticity, which is the process by which neurons rewire themselves by creating new connections. "What we demonstrate," says Just, "is that we can change the way the brain works. The study shows that we can make a brain area more active through remedial training."[51]

> " According to Sharon Berger, who is an optometrist and vision therapy specialist, eye problems that may not show up in routine vision screenings often result in children being misdiagnosed with learning disabilities. "

## Learning Disability or Vision Problems?

Learning disabilities are not related to mental retardation, poor hearing, or impaired vision, which is why children must be tested for such physical ailments before being diagnosed. But according to Sharon Berger, who is an optometrist and vision therapy specialist, eye problems that may not show up in routine vision screenings often result in children being misdiagnosed with learning disabilities. Although her theory is not endorsed by most physicians, Berger maintains that children who have 20-20 vision may still have a disconnect between what their eyes see and what registers in their brains. Leonard Press, who is with the College of Optometrists in Vision Development (of which Berger is a member), says that parents need to be aware of such conditions and question school officials who pronounce a child to be learning disabled. He explains: "You should be familiar with the warning signs of possible vision problems. Almost one child in four has vision problems that are significant enough to affect academic performance. Children often don't know that they are not seeing as well as they should. They don't know what they don't know."[52]

One child who was treated at Berger's clinic was McKay Shively, who had a severe reading problem when she was in elementary school. Whenever she tried to read she felt nauseated, which caused her to omit words, drop letters, and skip entire lines without realizing she was doing it. Berger determined that McKay suffered from a vision problem that impaired her depth perception and hand-eye coordination, both of which affected her reading and writing ability. After her weekly vision therapy sessions, her reading and writing skills began to improve.

## "Just Different"

Learning disabilities affect people of all ages, all walks of life, both genders, and all races and religions. They often cause frustration and a sense of failure for those who suffer from them, although with specialized education and treatment, many overcome their disabilities and achieve great success in life. As for the cause? There is much speculation about that, but at this point scientists can only theorize, as no definitive cause has ever been determined. Is there a cure? Not yet, but research has produced some exciting findings that may lead to a cure someday. In the meantime, people with learning disabilities must learn to live with them and do their best to capitalize on their strengths and compensate for their weaknesses. Robert Cimera shares his thoughts:

> Learning disabilities aren't . . . a curse from the Dark Ages. They aren't terminal or life threatening. They don't mean that your child or student is "stupid" or that he or she can't learn or will never succeed in life. Learning disabilities don't mean any of this. *Learning disability* is simply a term that indicates that a person processes information differently from what is considered the norm. . . . People such as myself have a difficult time processing what they are told. And so forth. It doesn't make us better or worse than anyone else, just different. And that's okay.[53]

# Can Learning Disabilities Be Cured?

Primary Source Quotes

**66** Learning disabilities (unlike developmental delays) are cognitive problems that are likely to continue throughout life. Learning disabilities can be managed but not 'cured.' **99**

—*District Administration*, "Understanding Learning Disabilities," August 2005.

*District Administration*, which is targeted at educational leaders, covers current trends and technological and leadership issues in the education industry.

**66** Learning disabilities are lifelong conditions that cannot be cured as some myths suggest. **99**

—Paula Ketter, "The Hidden Disability," *T+D*, June 2006. www.worksourcewi.com.

Ketter is managing editor of *T+D*, a publication of the American Society for Training & Development.

* Editor's Note: While the definition of a primary source can be narrowly or broadly defined, for the purposes of Compact Research, a primary source consists of: 1) results of original research presented by an organization or researcher; 2) eyewitness accounts of events, personal experience, or work experience; 3) first-person editorials offering pundits' opinions; 4) government officials presenting political plans and/or policies; 5) representatives of organizations presenting testimony or policy.

66 No matter how many times it's been said, it needs to be repeated again and again: learning disabilities do not go away, and LD is a problem with lifelong implications. 99

—Sheldon H. Horowitz, "Research Roundup: Learning Disabilities in Adulthood—the Struggle Continues," *LD News*, March 2006. www.ncld.org.

Horowitz is the director of professional services at the National Center for Learning Disabilities.

66 Imagine a future where students who have diverse learning needs will have the opportunity to learn and love learning. 99

—Don Johnston, "Learning Alternatives and Strategies for Students Who Are Struggling," *Exceptional Parent*, September 2008.

Johnston, who struggled with a learning disability throughout much of his life, is founder and CEO of a company that develops instructional materials for students with special needs.

66 People with learning disabilities have a significantly lower life expectancy than people without; a significant factor in this is health and lifestyle problems, which in people without learning disabilities would ordinarily be identified and dealt with, going unrecognised and untreated. 99

—Alan Johnson, "Speech by Rt Hon Alan Johnson," National Children and Adult Services Conference, October 24, 2008. www.dh.gov.uk.

Johnson is the United Kingdom's secretary of state for health.

66 **While there is no direct cure for a learning disability, early screening and intervention from specialists can often provide great benefits.** 99

—National Institute of Child Health and Human Development, "Learning Disabilities," February 23, 2007. www.nichd.nih.gov.

The National Institute of Child Health and Human Development conducts and supports research on topics related to the health of children, adults, families, and populations.

66 **There is no 'cure' for learning disabilities and learning disabilities cannot be treated with medication in the way ADHD can.** 99

—Learning Disabilities Association of New York State, "Learning Disabilities Defined," 2008. www.ldanys.org.

The Learning Disabilities Association of New York State exists to promote the education and general welfare of individuals with learning disabilities.

66 **If left untreated, learning disabilities may cause a lifetime of problems.** 99

—Ann Reyes, "Learning Disability," Discovery Health: Diseases and Conditions, November 30, 2006. http://health.discovery.com.

Reyes is a psychologist and medical writer.

# Can Learning Disabilities Be Cured?

- The majority of health-care professionals say that because learning disabilities are not a medical condition, they can be **treated but not cured**.

- By far the most common treatment for learning disabilities is **special education**.

- Research suggests that about **50 percent** of children with ADHD will no longer have the disorder by the time they reach puberty.

- Scientists say that unlike ADHD, people **do not grow out of learning disabilities**.

- The focus of current research is on developing techniques to diagnose and treat learning disabilities, as well as increasing understanding of the **biological basis**.

- Some learning disabilities may be treated with medications that **enhance a child's attention and ability to concentrate**, thus helping him or her learn.

- Studies have shown that the younger children are when they begin treatment for learning disabilities, the more **successful** the treatment will be.

# Can Learning Disabilities Be Cured?

Although scientists say that there is no specific cure for learning disabilities, some studies have revealed that with the right treatment program, people achieve such remarkable progress that they are no longer learning-impaired. One research project published in August 2008 showed that after intensive reading instruction, children with dyslexia exhibited barely any sign of a neurological disorder. From this the scientists concluded that it is possible to rewire the brains of some learning-disabled people. These illustrations depict brain scans of the students involved in the study before and after the therapy.

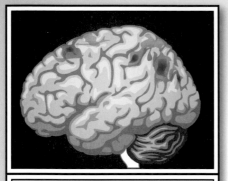

Pre-remediation brain scan—regions of the brain (shown in red) are underactivated in dyslexic readers

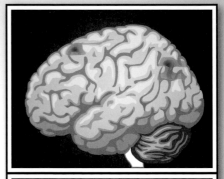

Brain scan after 100 hours of remedial reading instruction—underactive regions much less pronounced

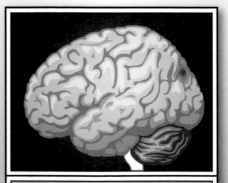

Brain scan at one year follow-up—underactive regions are largely eliminated

Source: Physorg, "Remedial Instruction Rewires Dyslexic Brains, Provides Lasting Results, Study Shows," August 5, 2008. www.physorg.com.

# Treating Learning Disabilities with Drugs

Whether prescription medications should be used to treat learning disabilities is a controversial issue. Many health-care professionals say that drugs are not effective in helping people overcome their learning challenges; rather, they say that specialized education is the more appropriate treatment. This graph shows the percent of children and youth aged 6 to 17 with learning disabilities and/or attention deficit hyperactivity disorder (ADHD) who used prescription drugs as treatment.

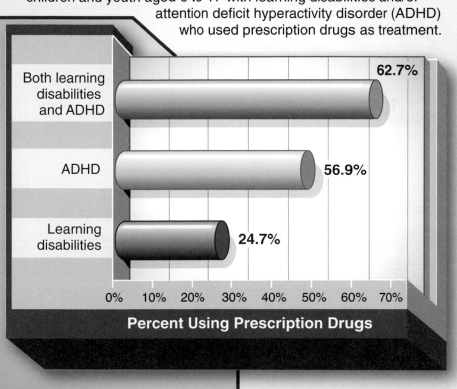

Source: Patricia N. Pastor and Cynthia A. Reuben, "Diagnosed Attention Deficit Hyperactivity Disorder and Learning Disability, United States, 2004–2006," CDC, July 2008. www.cdc.gov.

- In 2005 researchers from the University of California–Los Angeles announced that a drug called **Lovastatin** could potentially correct the cognitive defects that are thought to be connected with learning disabilities.

# Educating Special-Needs Children

Even in the absence of a distinct cure for learning disabilities, specialized education has been shown to help the learning-disabled make such excellent progress that many overcome their learning challenges. According to the U.S. Department of Education, a larger number of children and youth aged 3 to 21 have received special education for learning disabilities than for any other type of disability.

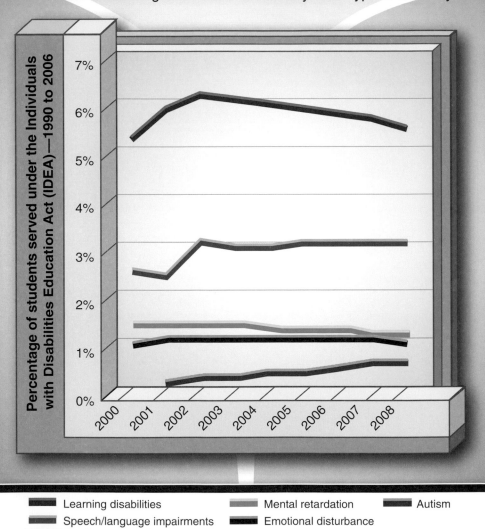

Learning disabilities
Speech/language impairments
Mental retardation
Emotional disturbance
Autism

Source: National Center for Education Statistics, "The Condition of Education 2008," June 2008. http://nces.ed.gov.

- **Fragile X syndrome** is a genetic disorder that has been linked to learning disabilities and mental retardation. In October 2008 researchers from the University of California–Irvine announced that when they injected the brains of genetically altered mice with a protein involved in neural growth, the creatures' cognitive functions showed improvement.

# Key People and Advocacy Groups

**Rudolf Berlin:** A German ophthalmologist who coined the term *dyslexia* in 1877.

**Tom Cruise:** A well-known actor who has struggled with dyslexia throughout his life.

**Jarron Draper:** A young man who made national headlines when a court ruled that Atlanta Public Schools must pay for four years of private schooling after erroneously diagnosing him as mentally retarded in 1998.

**International Dyslexia Association:** A scientific and educational organization dedicated to the study and treatment of dyslexia and other language-based learning disabilities.

**Samuel Kirk:** A psychologist who first used the term *learning disabilities* in a book published in 1962.

**Adolf Kussmaul:** A German physician who published an article in 1877 in which he described the unusual disorder of one of his adult patients as "word blindness."

**Learning Disabilities Association of America:** An organization that seeks to create opportunities for success for everyone who is affected by learning disabilities as well as reduce the incidence of learning disabilities in future generations.

**Jim Myers:** A teacher, coach, and former professional wrestler who earned advanced college degrees after struggling his entire life with a learning disability.

**National Center for Learning Disabilities (NCLD):** NCLD's mission is to ensure that America's children, adolescents, and adults with learning disabilities have every opportunity to succeed in school, work, and life.

**National Dissemination Center for Children with Disabilities:** A government health agency that provides information on issues such as child and youth disabilities, programs and services, and special education laws.

**National Institute of Neurological Disorders and Stroke:** A federal government organization that seeks to reduce the burden of neurological disease throughout the world through research and education.

**Gavin Newsom:** The mayor of San Francisco, Newsom struggled with dyslexia for years and eventually overcame it.

**Charles Schwab:** After overcoming dyslexia Schwab went on to found the largest brokerage firm in the United States and became a well-known advocate for people with learning disabilities.

**Sally E. Shaywitz and Bennett A. Shaywitz:** Researchers who have extensively studied dyslexia and determined the regions of the brain where it originates.

# Chronology

**1877**
German physician Adolf Kussmaul publishes an article in which he uses the term *word blindness* to describe one of his patients with a severe reading deficiency.

**1969**
The U.S. Congress passes the Children with Specific Learning Disabilities Act, marking the first time federal law mandates educational support services for learning-disabled children.

**1905**
The first U.S. report of childhood reading difficulties is published by W.E. Bruner, an ophthalmologist from Cleveland, Ohio.

**1962**
In his book *Educating Exceptional Children*, psychologist Samuel Kirk introduces the term *learning disabilities* to describe deficiencies in the language, speech, reading, and communication skills needed for social interaction.

1850    1950    1960    1970

**1887**
German ophthalmologist Rudolf Berlin coins the term *dyslexia* to describe a reading disorder.

**1963**
A conference in Chicago is hosted by a group of parents whose common bond is their special-needs children; as a keynote speaker, Samuel Kirk shares with them the term *learning disabilities*.

**1964**
The parent group that hosted the Chicago conference forms the Association for Children with Learning Disabilities and begins lobbying for their children to receive specialized help in school; later the organization's name is changed to the Learning Disabilities Association of America.

**1937**
After observing reading difficulties in children, especially those that involve words and letters to be reversed or transposed, American physician Samuel Orton names the condition strephosymbolia, meaning "twisted symbols."

**1975**
With congressional passage of the Education of All Handicapped Children Act, all students aged 3 to 21 with special needs are guaranteed a free and appropriate public education and the right to learn in regular classrooms along with students who are not learning disabled.

**2009**
In experiments with mice a team of Canadian researchers shows a direct link between a brain protein known as Neto1 and learning disabilities and is able to reverse the deficiencies using experimental drugs.

**2008**
A federal appeals court upholds a ruling that Atlanta Public Schools must pay $152,000 for private schooling for Jarron Draper, who had been diagnosed by the school system as mentally retarded in 1998.

**1990**
The Education of All Handicapped Children Act is renamed the Individuals with Disabilities Education Act (IDEA).

1975    1990    2000                                    2010

**2001**
A study published in the *Journal of Learning Disabilities* shows that the prevalence of dyscalculia is nearly 10 times higher in families where one (or more) individual suffers from the disorder than in the general population.

**2005**
The U.S. surgeon general releases an advisory warning pregnant women to abstain from alcohol because of potential risks to the fetus, including learning disabilities.

**2007**
After using functional magnetic resonance imaging to scan the brains of dyslexic and nondyslexic patients, researchers Sally E. and Bennett A. Shaywitz determine several areas of the brain where dyslexia originates.

# Related Organizations

### Children and Adults with Attention-Deficit/Hyperactivity Disorder (CHADD)

8181 Professional Pl., Suite 150
Landover, MD 20785
phone: (301) 306-7070; toll-free: (800) 233-4050
fax: (301) 306-7090
e-mail: nrc@chadd.org • Web site: www.chadd.org

CHADD provides education, advocacy, and support for individuals who have attention-deficit/hyperactivity disorder. A variety of information is available on its Web site, including reports, research studies, frequently asked questions, and facts about ADHD causes, symptoms, and treatment.

### Council for Learning Disabilities (CLD)

11184 Antioch Rd., Box 405
Overland Park, KS 66210
phone: (913) 491-1011 • fax: (913) 491-1012
e-mail: cldinfo@ie-events.com • Web site: www.cldinternational.org

CLD promotes evidence-based teaching, collaboration, research, leadership, and advocacy for people with learning disabilities. Its Web site features the *LD Forum* newsletter, federal legislation information, a paper about students with learning disabilities, and links to related Web sites.

### International Dyslexia Association (IDA)

40 York Rd., 4th Floor
Baltimore, MD 21204
phone: (410) 296-0232 • fax: (410) 321-5069
e-mail: info@interdys.org • Web site: www.interdys.org

IDA is a scientific and educational organization dedicated to the study and treatment of dyslexia and other language-based learning disabilities. Its Web site features fact sheets, frequently asked questions, an e-newsletter, and an online bookstore.

## Learning Disabilities Association of America (LDA)

4156 Library Rd.
Pittsburgh, PA 15234-1349
phone: (412) 341-1515 • fax: (412) 344-0224
e-mail: info@ldaamerica.org • Web site: www.ldaamerica.org

LDA seeks to create opportunities for success for everyone who is affected by learning disabilities, as well as reduce the incidence of learning disabilities in future generations. A number of position papers are available on its Web site, along with numerous guides and booklets, legislative updates, and links to other learning disability organizations.

## National Academy for Child Development (NACD)

549 Twenty-fifth St.
Ogden, UT 84401
phone: (801) 621-8606 • fax: (801) 621-8389
e-mail: info@nacd.org • Web site: www.nacd.org

NACD is a family-centered organization that provides neurodevelopmental evaluations and individualized programs for children and adults. Available on its Web site are numerous articles, a newsletter (including archives), press releases, and testimonials from parents whose children have benefited from NACD services.

## National Association of Special Education Teachers (NASET)

1250 Connecticut Ave. NW, Suite 200
Washington, DC 20036
phone and fax: (800) 754-4421
e-mail: contactus@naset.org • Web site: www.naset.org

NASET was founded to promote the profession of special education teachers and to provide a national forum for their ideas. Its Web site features numerous publications, including an introduction to learning disabilities, as well as papers on literacy, legislation, and other issues.

### National Center for Learning Disabilities (NCLD)

381 Park Ave. S., Suite 1401
New York, NY 10016
phone: (212) 545-7510; toll-free: (888) 575-7373
fax: (212) 545-9665
Web site: www.ld.org

NCLD seeks to ensure that America's children, adolescents, and adults with learning disabilities have every opportunity to succeed in school, work, and life. A wealth of information is available on its Web site, including a "Teen Topics" section, numerous facts about various learning disabilities, the monthly *LD News* newsletter, transcripts of interviews with learning disability experts, and statistics.

### National Dissemination Center for Children with Disabilities (NICHCY)

PO Box 1492
Washington, DC 20013
phone: (800) 695-0285; toll-free: (800) 695-0285
fax: (202) 884-8441
e-mail: nichcy@aed.org • Web site: www.nichcy.org

NICHCY provides information on issues such as child and youth disabilities, programs and services, and special education laws. Its Web site features a collection of fact sheets, research summaries, details about federal legislation, special education and disability terms, and a wide variety of NICHCY publications.

### National Institute of Child Health and Human Development (NICHD)

Bldg. 31, Room 2A32, MSC 2425
31 Center Dr.
Bethesda, MD 20892-2425
phone: (800) 370-2943 • fax: (866) 760-5947
e-mail: nichdinformationresourcecenter@mail.nih.gov
Web site: www.nichd.nih.gov

NICHD conducts and supports research on topics related to the health of children, adults, families, and populations. Its Web site features "A to Z health and human development topics," as well as a variety of articles about learning disabilities.

## National Institute of Mental Health (NIMH)

Science Writing, Press, and Dissemination Branch
6001 Executive Blvd., Room 8184, MSC 9663
Bethesda, MD 20892-9663
phone: (301) 443-4513; toll-free: (866) 615-6464
fax: (301) 443-4279
e-mail: nimhinfo@nih.gov • Web site: www.nimh.nih.gov

NIMH envisions a world in which mental illnesses can be prevented and cured, and its mission is to transform the understanding and treatment of mental illnesses through basic and clinical research. The search engine on its Web site produces a large number of articles about the various learning disabilities, including what they are and how they are diagnosed and treated.

## National Institute of Neurological Disorders and Stroke (NINDS)

PO Box 5801
Bethesda, MD 20824
phone: (301) 496-5751; toll-free: (800) 352-9424
fax: (301) 402-2060
Web site: www.ninds.nih.gov

NINDS, which is part of the National Institutes of Health, seeks to reduce the burden of neurological disease throughout the world through research and education. A number of publications are available on its Web site, including news articles, research papers, and general information about learning disorders.

# For Further Research

## Books
Robert Evert Cimera, *Learning Disabilities: What Are They?* Lanham, MD: Rowman & Littlefield, 2007.

Brock Eide and Fernette Eide, *The Mislabeled Child.* New York: Hyperion, 2006.

Joan M. Harwell and Rebecca Williams Jackson, *The Complete Learning Disabilities Handbook.* San Francisco: Wiley, 2008.

Grant Martin, *Help! My Child Is Struggling in School.* Carol Stream, IL: Tyndale House, 2006.

Jonathan Mooney: *The Short Bus: A Journey Beyond Normal.* New York: Holt, 2007.

Carol Turkington, *Encyclopedia of Learning Disabilities.* New York: Facts On File, 2006.

Rich Weinfeld et al., *Smart Kids with Learning Disabilities.* Waco, TX: Prufrock, 2006.

Bernice Y.L. Wong, ed., *Learning About Learning Disabilities.* San Diego, CA: Elsevier Academic, 2004.

## Periodicals
Bernadette Angle, "Winning the 'Game' Against Learning Disabilities," *Coach and Athletic Director*, September 2007.

Christen Brownlee, "Statins for Algernon: Cholesterol-Lowering Drug Fights Learning Disability," *Science News*, November 12, 2005.

*Career World: A Weekly Reader Publication*, "The Gift of a Learning Difference," February/March 2009.

Diane Cole, "Learning with a Difference," *U.S. News & World Report*, August 27, 2007.

Jan Farrington, "The Invisible Disability: Teens Tackle Learning Disabilities," *Current Health 2: A Weekly Reader Publication*, October 2008.

Sean McCollum, "Decoding Dyslexia," *Scholastic Choices*, October 2006.

Jean M. McIntire, "Developing Literacy Through Music," *Teaching Music*, August 2007.

Bob Meadows, "Learning to Let Go," *People Weekly*, March 20, 2006.

H. Resnick, "Helicopter Mom Lets Go," *Toronto Globe & Mail*, February 5, 2009.

Morgan Wampler, "Teens with Learning Disabilities Have Some Help," *Roanoke (VA) Times*, February 4, 2009.

## Internet Sources

Centers for Disease Control and Prevention, *Diagnosed Attention Deficit Hyperactivity Disorder and Learning Disability: United States, 2004–2006*, July 2008. www.cdc.gov/nchs/data/series/sr_10/sr10_237.pdf.

Gary Direnfeld, "My Child Is Odd," Boloji, November 26, 2006. www.boloji.com/parenting/02335.htm.

Richard S. Kingsley, "What Is ADHD?" KidsHealth, September 2008. http://kidshealth.org/parent/medical/learning/adhd.html.

D'Arcy Lyness, "Learning Disabilities," TeensHealth, March 2007. http://kidshealth.org/teen/diseases_conditions/learning/learning_disabilities.html.

MedicineNet, "Learning Disabilities," July 31, 2008. www.medicinenet.com/learning_disability/article.htm.

Merck, "Learning Disabilities," November 2005. www.merck.com/mmpe/sec19/ch299/ch299d.html.

Bob Myers, "About Learning Disabilities," HealthyPlace, December 20, 2008. www.healthyplace.com/adhd/add-focus/about-learning-disabilities/print/menu-id-1584.

National Center for Learning Disabilities, "LD Basics." www.ncld.org/content/view/447/391.

PBS, *Misunderstood Minds*, 2002. www.pbs.org/wgbh/misunderstoodminds.

Ann Reyes, "Learning Disability," Discovery Health: Diseases and Conditions, November 30, 2006. http://health.discovery.com/encyclopedias/illnesses.html?chrome=None&article=2894&page=1.

# Source Notes

## Overview

1. Robert Evert Cimera, *Learning Disabilities: What Are They?* Lanham, MD: Rowman & Littlefield, 2007, p. 4.
2. Dawn D. Matthews, ed., *Learning Disabilities Sourcebook*. Detroit: Omnigraphics, p. 5.
3. Quoted in Matthews, *Learning Disabilities Sourcebook*, p. 4.
4. Quoted in Sheldon Horowitz, "Guiding Teens with Learning Disabilities: An Interview with Dr. Arlyn Roffman," National Center for Learning Disabilities, 2007. www.ncld.org.
5. Alison Rhodes, "The Beginning of My Journey with Learning Disabilities," The Safety Mom Chronicles: Learning Disabilities, September 1, 2008. http://blog.thesafetychronicles.com.
6. Cimera, *Learning Disabilities*, p. 128.
7. Cimera, *Learning Disabilities*, p. 190.
8. Cimera, *Learning Disabilities*, p. 64.
9. Darcy Andries, "ADHD and Learning Disabilities," Suite101, August 22, 2006. http://addadhd.suite101.com.
10. Andries, "ADHD and Learning Disabilities."
11. Gary Direnfeld, "My Child Is Odd," Bolojj, November 26, 2006. www.boloji.com.
12. Cimera, *Learning Disabilities*, p. 33.
13. Quoted in Heather Knight, "Newsom Comes Out: He's Dyslexic," *San Francisco Chronicle*, April 21, 2004. www.sfgate.com.
14. Quoted in Knight, "Newsom Comes Out."
15. National Dissemination Center for Children with Disabilities, "Learning Disabilities (LD)." www.nichcy.org.

## What Are Learning Disabilities?

16. Quoted in H. von Ziemssen and J.A.T. McCreery, eds., *Cyclopedia of the Practice of Medicine*. New York: William Wood, 1877, p. 770.
17. Quoted in Daniel P. Hallahan, "Learning Disabilities: Historical Perspectives," National Research Center on Learning Disabilities, November 19, 2007. www.nrcld.org.
18. U.S. Congress, "Public Law 108-446," December 3, 2004. www.nichcy.org.
19. Cimera, *Learning Disabilities*, p. 77.
20. Tom Cruise, "My Struggle to Read," *People*, July 21, 2003. www.people.com.
21. Cruise, "My Struggle to Read."
22. Cimera, *Learning Disabilities*, p. 80.
23. Cimera, *Learning Disabilities*, p. 83.
24. Leane Somers, "Learning Disabilities: Recognizing Dysgraphia in Children with ADHD," *ADDitude*. www.additudemag.com.
25. Cimera, *Learning Disabilities*, p. 106.

## What Causes Learning Disabilities?

26. Larry B. Silver, "What You Must Know to Understand Learning Disabilities," eNotAlone. www.enotalone.com.
27. Matthews, *Learning Disabilities Sourcebook*, p. 10.
28. Quoted in *LabNews*, "Study Is Breakthrough for Dyscalculia Sufferers," April 2007. www.labnews.co.uk.
29. Sally E. Shaywitz and Bennett A. Shaywitz, "The Neurobiology of Reading and Dyslexia," *Focus on Basics*, November 2007. www.ncsall.net.
30. Quoted in Office of the Surgeon General, "U.S. Surgeon General Releases Advisory on Alcohol Use in Preg-

nancy," February 21, 2005. www.surgeongeneral.gov.

31. Office of the Surgeon General, "U.S. Surgeon General Releases Advisory on Alcohol Use in Pregnancy."

32. *ScienceDaily*, "Marijuana and Alcohol Taken Together Induced Widespread Nerve Cell Death in Brains of Young Rats," April 11, 2008. www.sciencedaily.com.

33. Quoted in Angela Haupt, "It's Banned but Not Gone: Lead Paint Is Still a Danger," *USA Today*, August 28, 2007. www.usatoday.com.

34. National Association of Special Education Teachers, "Theoretical Perspectives on the Causes of Learning Disabilities," 2006/2007. www.naset.org.

## Can People Overcome Learning Disabilities?

35. Quoted in Kirsten Stewart, "Sandy Teen Overcomes Learning Disability," *Salt Lake Tribune*, February 25, 2009. www.sltrib.com.

36. Stewart, "Sandy Teen Overcomes Learning Disability."

37. Brock Eide and Fernette Eide, *The Mislabeled Child*. New York: Hyperion, 2006, p. 19.

38. Eide and Eide, *The Mislabeled Child*, p. 5.

39. Jenifer Fox, "Causes of Learning Disabilities," SelfGrowth, February 23, 2009. www.selfgrowth.com.

40. Fox, "Causes of Learning Disabilities."

41. Don C. Johnston, "Learning Alternatives and Strategies for Students Who Are Struggling," *Exceptional Parent*, September 2008, p. 9.

42. Johnston, "Learning Alternatives and Strategies for Students Who Are Struggling."

43. Quoted in Diane Cole, "Need Extra Help? Just Ask," *U.S. News & World Report*, August 21, 2008. www.usnews.com.

44. Quoted in Cole, "Need Extra Help? Just Ask."

## Can Learning Disabilities Be Cured?

45. National Institute of Mental Health, "Learning Disabilities Reversed in Mice," November 25, 2008. www.nimh.nih.gov.

46. National Institute of Mental Health, "Learning Disabilities Reversed in Mice."

47. National Institute of Mental Health, "Learning Disabilities Reversed in Mice."

48. Quoted in Eureka! Science, "Study of Learning Disabled Mice Shows Balance in the Brain Is Key," October 30, 2008. http://esciencenews.com.

49. Quoted in *Record*, "Canadian Researchers Link Brain Protein with Learning Disabilities," February 24, 2009. http://news.therecord.com.

50. Ker Than, "Brain Cells Colored to Create 'Brainbow,'" LiveScience, October 31, 2007. www.livescience.com.

51. Quoted in Tom Valeo, "Dyslexia Studies Catch Neuroplasticity at Work," Dana Foundation, November 1, 2008. http://dana.org.

52. Quoted in Bill Hendrick, "Eye Therapy Fixes Misdiagnosed Learning Disabilities, Backers Say," *Seattle Post-Intelligencer*, October 21, 2004.

53. Cimera, *Learning Disabilities*, p. 191.

# List of Illustrations

List of Illustrations

# Index

# About the Author

Peggy J. Parks holds a bachelor of science degree from Aquinas College in Grand Rapids, Michigan, where she graduated magna cum laude. She has written more than 80 nonfiction educational books for children and young adults, as well as self-publishing her own cookbook called *Welcome Home: Recipes, Memories, and Traditions from the Heart*. Parks lives in Muskegon, Michigan, a town that she says inspires her writing because of its location on the shores of Lake Michigan.